Praise for Mirco Hering and

DevOps for the Modern Enterprise

Mirco knows his stuff. He has a way of stating simple choices and framing options that encourage action. His unique perspective on how to transform your IT organization, especially when you have heavily invested in outsourcing, are both thoughtful and practical. After you read his book, make sure to subscribe to his blog. You want to make sure to have Mirco by your side as you go through this transformation.

—**Mustafa Kapadia**, Digital Transformation Leader, IBM

This is a much-needed book on building teamwork to drive technology infrastructure efforts. Mirco introduces a simple set of processes and well-reasoned principles to align the organization, transform technology infrastructure, and deliver value for customers.

—**Eric Passmore**, Partner Director of Commerce at Microsoft

A pragmatic view on IT and DevOps that doesn't just focus on the "what" but the "how," based on firsthand experience.

—**Ajay Nair**, DevOps Architect, Accenture

This is a truly practical companion book to the other leading publications in the DevOps space. Mirco shares real-world lessons from many years of collective experience and provides tried and tested exercises for you to use to help drive insights and improvements in your organization.

—**Emily Arnautovic**, Software Architect, Accenture

DevOps is a hot topic. Pretty much every major organization wants it, and pretty much every major organization is struggling to come to grips with what "it" is and exactly how to get it. Mirco is a rare entity in the space. He's an architect who has grown up in large, complex organizations working with even larger, more complex systems integrators and delivery partners heavily reliant on ERP, CRM, and other COTS applications that seem to challenge much of what DevOps is about. Both pragmatic and practical, he not only gives great tips on how to find your way down the DevOps path in these environments but will help you avoid many a mistake as he shares his own.

—**Mark Richards**, SAFe Fellow at Coactivation

DevOps *for the* Modern Enterprise

DevOps *for the* Modern Enterprise

Winning Practices to Transform Legacy IT Organizations

Mirco Hering

**Foreword by
Dr. Bhaskar Ghosh**

IT Revolution
Portland, Oregon

25 NW 23rd Pl, Suite 6314
Portland, OR 97210

First Edition
Printed in the United States of America
24 23 22 21 19 18   1 2 3 4 5 6 7 8 9 10

Cover and book design by Devon Smith
Author photograph by Julian Dolman

Library of Congress Catalog-in-Publication Data

Names: Hering, Mirco, author.
Title: DevOps for the modern enterprise : winning practices to transform legacy IT organizations / Mirco Hering.
Description: First edition. | Portland, OR : IT Revolution Press, 2017. | Includes bibliographical references and index.
Identifiers: LCCN 2017053420 (print) | LCCN 2017056532 (ebook) | ISBN 9781942788201 (ePub) | ISBN 9781942788225 (Kindle) | ISBN 9781942788195 (trade pbk.)
Subjects: LCSH: Computer system conversion. | Operating systems (Computers) | Computer software--Development. | Management information systems. | Information technology—Management.
Classification: LCC QA76.9.C68 (ebook) | LCC QA76.9.C68 H47 2017 (print) | DDC 004.068—dc23
LC record available at https://lccn.loc.gov/2017053420

ISBN TP: 978-1942788195
ISBN ePub: 978-1942788201
ISBN Kindle: 978-1942788225
ISBN PDF: 978-1942788218

For information about special discounts for bulk purchases or for information on booking authors for an event, please visit our website at ITRevolution.com.

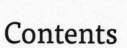

Contents

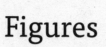

Figures

Chapter 5

Chapter 6

Chapter 7

Chapter 9

Chapter 10

Chapter 11

Chapter 12

Appendix

Tables

Chapter 1

Chapter 2

Chapter 3

Chapter 11

FOREWORD

by Dr. Bhaskar Ghosh

Throughout my many years working in the IT industry, I have encountered numerous disruptions from technology advances, new business models, and even global economic cycles. Among all those waves of change, DevOps in particular stands out. Paradoxically, it stands out not because of the principles it embodies but because of the downstream change it has ushered in.

I like to say that you can do DevOps without Agile, but you cannot do Agile without DevOps. This is just one of many examples of transformations that have been catalyzed by the advent of DevOps. By empowering software developers to do more and, consequently, own more, DevOps is unleashing creativity, which is leading to a feedback loop of continuous improvement in systems delivery.

While I fondly recall the time I spent years ago managing infrastructure operations for large enterprises, the challenges of that job often resulted from the distinction that was drawn between development and operations responsibilities. Of course, this was in an era of largely monolithic systems using Waterfall techniques for large-scale, periodic delivery of software releases. In those past production environments, such separation of duties was a practical and efficient operating model for the needed pace of system changes.

In the digital era, however, speed is paramount. The distinction of responsibilities is not conducive to the more incremental change delivery approaches that are required to meet the demands of business today.

In this book, Mirco shares much more than just the mechanics of DevOps; he also shares his passion for improving software engineering. Through clever analogies and prescriptive advice, Mirco dispenses practical recommendations for how to embrace DevOps in an enterprise. Whether you are just getting started with DevOps or you are a seasoned professional seeking counsel on how to apply its principles at scale, as you go through *DevOps for the Modern Enterprise*, you will find yourself infected by the enthusiasm Mirco has for DevOps and the benefits it can bring.

Dr. Bhaskar Ghosh
Group Chief Executive—Accenture Technology Services
Bangalore, India
March 2018

Preface

Learning is not compulsory; it's voluntary.
Improvement is not compulsory; it's voluntary.
But to survive, we must learn.

—W. Edwards Deming

One of the most rewarding things in my career has been the search to find the most efficient way to deliver meaningful projects and to get as many people as possible to do the same. When we are not working efficiently, we spend time on unnecessary, repetitive, and boring tasks, which is not fun at all. I don't have lofty goals of changing the world by doing my work, but I think everyone deserves to enjoy his or her work. And when workers enjoy what they do, good outcomes are inevitable.

Since joining Accenture as a consultant over ten years ago, I have worked with dozens of teams to increase their delivery capability through increased productivity or increased speed. But even before my time as a consultant, I was driven to figure out ways to bring efficiency to IT. I came into the workforce in the late 1990s when offshoring IT work was still in its early days. I spent my first few years as a developer in research labs for IBM, working on *telematics* and developer tools (e.g., developing languages for custom CPUs and providing the associated *compilers* and *IDE extensions*). When I started working, packaged software was on the rise, but most work was done in custom development and onshore. The only way to improve productivity was to increase the level of automation, and in all my early projects, we had creative solutions built around *shell scripts*, *Perl* scripts, and other custom tooling to make the life of developers and operators easier. I thoroughly enjoyed building these automation solutions and seeing how projects became easier and more enjoyable for everyone involved.

Then something curious happened. I spent the next five years on two large projects and focused on building the kind of developer tooling that I knew helped projects deliver successfully. When I finished those projects and started to look around across organizations, I realized that somehow I didn't see as much automation as I would have expected. After all, I spent all of my professional life working on automating tasks for delivery teams. When I spoke to others in the industry, it became clear that packaged software and offshore delivery capabilities provided shortcuts to productivity gains and cost reductions that many organizations leveraged rather than investing in good development practices and tooling.* I spent the next few years in what was perceived as a niche market to help organizations implement delivery tooling, but truth be told, it just wasn't sexy for organizations to invest in this.

Larger and larger offshore percentages and reductions of the average cost per developer workday (otherwise known as ADR, *average daily rate*) were targets that could more easily be sold to the organization as success than the somewhat more difficult and less easily measurable activity of developing a good delivery platform that makes everyone in IT more productive. After all, how do you measure productivity in IT in the first place? I am with Randy Shoup and Adrian Cockcroft, who both admitted while presenting at conferences that in their whole career, they have been looking for a good measure of productivity but have not been able

---

* For more information, see my DevOps.com article "Why We Are Still Fighting with the Same Problems in DevOps as 15 Years Ago."

to find something useful. I elaborated on this in a blog post to describe that productivity is very difficult to measure in IT; instead, measure cycle time, waste, and delivered functionality.[1] It is important to measure some meaningful metrics, as you are otherwise not able to see whether you are improving; it just turns out that productivity in the usual sense is elusive in IT and that we need to look for other measures that help us judge how efficient we are.

I spent the next few years working to understand where the problems in IT are coming from and how to solve them. I was lucky, as my research fell into a time when technology and methodology were evolving to bring out the foundations to a new way of delivering IT: Agile, DevOps, and *cloud*, among others, made it a lot easier to implement the kind of solutions I had built my entire career. The niche that I had worked in became more and more fashionable; today it is difficult to find an organization that is not talking about Agile and DevOps.

Yet when we take a good, hard look at ourselves in the mirror and see where the IT industry is currently, we realize that IT delivery is still not where it should be. We all tend to agree on *continuous delivery* being a good practice to use and to build modern application architectures, but when we look for organizations that have mastered it, they are few and far between. Many organizations are working in ways that have evolved over many years by taking lessons from traditional manufacturing. After all, those practices are well codified in many an MBA curriculum and have hundreds of years of experience behind them. But those practices and ideas are not appropriate anymore.

I have not mastered it all myself and am still learning every day and with every engagement, but I want to make my experiences available to as many people as possible. As you can see from Figure 0.1, I am a developer at heart who looked for technical solutions first instead of considering the people involved. I had to learn the hard way that just having the right methods and tools will not magically transform an organization. The

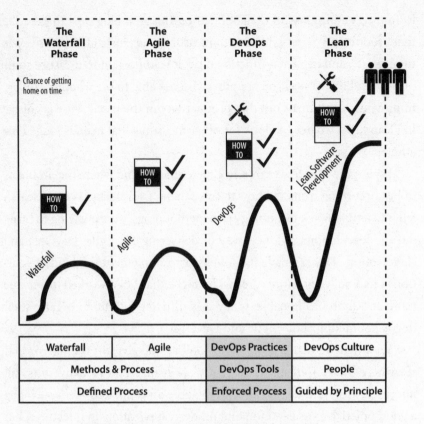

The Waterfall Phase • The Agile Phase • The DevOps Phase • The Lean Phase

Chance of getting home on time

HOW TO ✓

Waterfall

HOW TO ✓✓

Agile

HOW TO ✓✓

DevOps

HOW TO ✓✓

Lean Software Development

Waterfall	Agile	DevOps Practices	DevOps Culture
Methods & Process		DevOps Tools	People
Defined Process		Enforced Process	Guided by Principle

Figure 0.1: How Mirco's understanding of organizational change evolved

cultural change that is the hardest is also the most impactful. It took a good amount of failures and near misses to learn what I have to share in this book and to understand that you need to bring all the ingredients together with the right culture to really transform an organization.

Over the last few years, I have developed a workshop that I run with CIOs and other IT leadership from our clients to explore their challenges and help them identify possible ways forward. The fascinating thing when you are in a room with intelligent and visionary leaders is that you learn more each time. I have been running this workshop for a while, and I am extremely thankful for the experiences and ideas that the CIOs have shared with me, which continue to improve the workshop. (This book contains the accumulated knowledge from those sessions.)

DevOps for the Modern Enterprise is meant to address the different challenges that organizations face as they transform into modern IT organizations, and yes, most organizations today are IT organizations, whether they are car manufacturers or banks, due to the dependence on IT for their core business. We all know that technology is evolving faster and faster. In the meantime, we have *legacy* applications from many years ago. Even new applications that we are building today will be legacy in a few years' time. I actually subscribe to the idea that legacy is any code written before today. Software and technology are transforming the business landscape by enabling new ways for people to connect, share, and collaborate. Furthermore, technology has freed people from constraints and geography. As a result, the world is becoming more complex and even faster, and these new consumption patterns are disrupting well-established business practices. Many organizations are facing the fundamental challenge of modernizing their IT infrastructure. Our old *mental models* and methods are clearly not working anymore. We need new ways of dealing with the need for new solutions. The path toward modernized solutions and improved technology remains mysterious and tricky. Very few legacy organizations have mastered the transformation.

Over the years, I've worked with some of the largest technology organizations in every industry vertical. And whatever excuses you may have, whether they're about technology, complexity, or culture, I claim that I've seen worse. And yet, these organizations have been able to radically transform and improve their outcomes. I want to share some of their learning and achievements with you. IT should not be a place where we spend the majority of time solving the same old problems again and again.

Everything in this book is supported by Agile, DevOps, and Lean principles. In fact, I start pretty much all my client discussions by asking "What do these principles mean to you?" because they are all so ambiguous. I tend to use the overview picture in Figure 0.2 to make sure everyone understands exactly how I use these principles.

The mission I've set for myself as an advisor to my clients is to make myself redundant. Once my clients are leveraging the principles of Lean, DevOps, and Agile successfully and are working in an efficient way, I can go off and spend more time on implementing exciting solutions. I cannot think of a better goal in life than to make myself redundant and go on to focus on one or two projects instead.

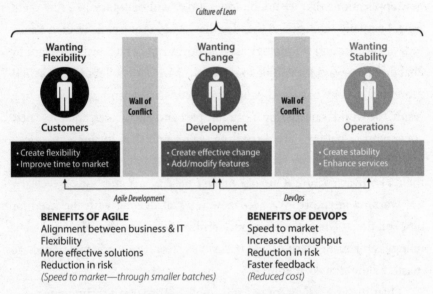

Figure 0.2: Relationship between Agile and DevOps: How the principles Lean, Agile, and DevOps relate to each other

But as long as IT continues to be a place where too many things go wrong and where people struggle every day, I will help make IT a better place to be. I will aim to help the transition with this book, as my team cannot be everywhere. There is more than enough work for all of us. Like all honest answers to complex problems, this is just a starting point. You should feel free to experiment with the recipe, add your own ingredients, and shake it up. Each journey of transformation is contextual, and there is never only one recipe for success.

I hope that with this book I can make it easier for all of you to navigate the challenges ahead. I am sharing my experience and practical exercises that I run with my clients and that you can use in your organization (whether small or large, old or new) to progress in your journey. I am looking forward to seeing you along the journey: at a conference talking about our successes and failures, at a meet-up over drinks, or perhaps on one of my consulting engagements as we solve some challenges together.

I am a developer at heart, and I want to develop cool new applications. Let's transform our industry so that we can all spend more time on the creative side of IT.

Mirco Hering

INTRODUCTION

How We Got Here

The greatest danger in times of turbulence is not the turbulence;
it is to act with yesterday's logic.
—**Peter F. Drucker**, *Managing in Turbulent Times*

Before we get into the meat of the book, I want to take a moment to explain why it is so important to change the way we approach IT delivery. We obviously didn't choose to be in the situation we are in today, where most organizations are struggling to deliver IT in a way that truly supports the business. IT is either too slow or too expensive, or does not deliver the quality that business stakeholders expect, but it's not because we have consciously made bad decisions. When you look around, we are also pretty much in agreement as to what good looks like—the examples of Netflix or Google are used in literally hundreds of presentations about IT. Pretty much every organization is talking about Agile and flexible delivery, automation across the *software delivery life cycle* (SDLC), and leveraging modern architecture patterns like *cloud native application*, *twelve-factor applications*, and *microservices*.

Yet if we look around, we still struggle to find organizations that have mastered this new way of working in IT. Many of the organizations with good examples are relatively young organizations that have grown up as cloud or *internet natives* (companies that were founded with the internet as the target platform). We even have a term for them: DevOps unicorns. We call them unicorns because they are rare and seemingly unattainable for the average organization with a legacy IT architecture.

One could conclude that the challenge must be with this legacy architecture that organizations try to transform. While this is to some degree correct, I think it has even more to do with the mind-set. Many technology leaders are using ideas that were adopted from a traditional manufacturing context even though IT is inherently different*—they leverage the mental model of manufacturing for an inherently creative process. In traditional manufacturing, we follow a predictable process to produce the same outcome (a product) again and again. In contrast, we never do the same project twice in IT. To support this more creative nature of IT, we need to address three areas to achieve a shift in mind-set: the organizational ecosystem we find ourselves in, the people we work with, and the technologies that support our business. I have structured the book around these three dimensions. Here in the introduction, I will make the case for why the old mental model is not appropriate anymore. I will then spend the body of the book, which is organized into three parts, helping you transform your organization and adapt your mental models.

The three parts of the book are broken down as follows:

1. Part A: Creating the right ecosystem for success (chapters 1–4): How do you create an organization in which modern IT is possible? How do you work with other organizations such as software vendors and system integrators to support a new way of IT delivery? The first "meaty" part of the book goes into these kinds of questions and is really addressed to the CIO and other leaders in IT who set the strategy of the organization.

---

* Some DevOps books, like *The Phoenix Project*, leverage a modern manufacturing model that is different to the traditional model I am referring to.

2. Part B: The people dimension (chapters 5–8): Nothing happens in organizations without people. How little we sometimes consider this is reflected in our usage of the term "resources" instead of people. Part B of the book will focus on people and what we can do to empower people to bring their best to work each day, which will, in turn, make your organization more successful.

3. Part C: Technology in the driver's seat (chapters 9–12): There is no doubt in my mind that the recent advances in technology have made some of the new ways of working possible and are forcing leaders in the industry to rethink the way to deliver IT solutions. I will talk about some of the key trends and how best to leverage these. Technology is evolving ever more quickly, so I will refrain from using specific names of tools, vendors, or methods. For some help navigating this space, I will, however, provide a list of resources that I hope remains available and updated over time on the internet.

For each chapter in the main section of the book, there is a discussion of the topic in which we explore the problem space and what possible solutions and approaches can be used. I aim to keep the chapters short so that you can consume them in bite-size pieces.

At the end of each chapter, I provide exercises in the spirit of "how to try this at home," in which I present some practical steps for you to take to leverage what I have said in the chapter for your organizations. This will sometimes include templates, some questions to ask yourself or your organizations, or a step-by-step guide. It will not replace having someone with experience as an advisor but will provide you with some first steps to help you along the transformation journey.

I will also (somewhat self-indulgently) provide links to some of my blog posts along the way, usually when I have written more extensively about a topic but don't think it fits into the flow of this book. Feel free to check out those posts.

I've included a conclusion to wrap up the book and leave you with some general recommendations on how to take the next step. In addition, I've added my personal recipe for dealing with the demands of the fast speed in our industry. In all, the information found in this book should leave you feeling prepared to begin the transformation into a modern IT organization.

Finally, I've included an appendix that goes into more detail of the factory analogy I discuss throughout the book. If you're not familiar with it, you may want to read this appendix first, before moving into the meat of the book. For those who are well versed in the analogy, the appendix will provide a deeper understanding of it and help to further your thinking in this area. Let's quickly look at why a traditional manufacturing mind-set stands in the way of achieving the speed and reliability of IT delivery we are aiming for with DevOps.

Manufacturing Principles Don't Apply Easily to IT Delivery

In recent years, modern manufacturing has been the inspiration for many positive trends, like Lean, systems thinking, and theory of constraints. The Toyota manufacturing system, in fact, was one of the inspirations behind Agile and DevOps ideas. Yet many managers operate with a mental model that is more inspired by a legacy view of manufacturing—the image of manufacturing from the Henry Ford era. This factory model is based on the idea that we create a production process that allows us to put the intelligence into the process; then we can use less-skilled people to achieve a high-quality outcome. This is not true for IT work, where collaboration and creativeness are required to achieve the best outcomes. I believe that the principles of legacy manufacturing are causing many of the problems we currently see in legacy IT: rigid processes with a command-and-control mind-set; bloated, functionally specialized organizational structures; and large amounts of handovers that reduce the flow of work and increase the opportunities to introduce defects.

I chose the phrase "not a factory anymore" for my blog as a rallying cry for the change in thinking that IT executives need to make if they want to successfully transform their organization. The word "factory" in this phrase stands for the kind of factory Henry Ford represents, where mass manufacturing takes place with highly specialized people working on assembly lines to do a specific job and produce a mass product with little to no customizations.

Legacy manufacturing was based on the invention of the assembly line at Ford and the work that Frederick Taylor did on scientific management.[†] Building a factory was an expensive and time-consuming business. The work itself was optimized so that workers could become highly specialized at one specific task and do that task extremely efficiently. To reduce cost, a manufacturer had few choices: he could automate more by investing in better machines, he could change the material going into the product, and he could move his factory somewhere where the worker is paid less. Most changes to the product or production process would be a significant endeavor, as they required the purchase of new machines, reconfiguration of machines, teaching of new processes to all the workers, or a change in supply chains for the product material.

The product itself was not customizable (Henry Ford allegedly said about the Model T, "You can have any color as long as it's black"), so it was very easy to compare output and cost of the product. If you changed the production process or used different material for the product, you could evaluate the result scientifically (which is the idea that Taylor's work was

---

[†] Frederick Taylor is considered the founder of scientific management, which he implemented especially in the steel industry. He published *The Principles of Scientific Management* in 1911.

inspired by). One can argue that most of manufacturing today still allows you to do these kinds of measurements of cost and productivity, as most products are mass produced. This is the kind of manufacturing example that most economic education and, therefore, management is based upon. I went to university over fifteen years ago and did an MBA recently, so I know firsthand that most of the teaching of IT processes is still influenced by this model. It is, after all, relatively easy to understand and to control, which makes scientific treatment of the process possible.

You will see that IT in the early days had a lot in common with a manufacturing business. Let's put ourselves back in the 1990s at the IT department of a car company. (I like this scenario because I used to work in such a department during my school holidays and, based on that experience, was inspired to pursue a career in IT.) IT worked pretty similarly and had undergone similar trends as manufacturing had. Building a new IT system was an expensive and time-consuming business. The work itself was optimized so that workers could become highly specialized as testers; Java developers, SAP configurators, or operations engineers. Each one could focus on one specific task and do that extremely efficiently within an overall *Waterfall*-inspired SDLC process.

To reduce cost, the IT department had a few choices: they could automate more by investing in better tools, they could change the kind of software being used (for example, from custom Java to SAP to leverage existing functionality instead of building it), and later on, they could shift development or other functions somewhere where the worker is paid less. Most changes to the product after the design phase would be a significant endeavor, as this required changes to the contract with software vendors or significant rework for the existing team.

The product itself was pretty standard: an enterprise *resource planning (ERP) system* or a *customer relationship management (CRM) system* using "best practices" coming from packaged solutions. And while it was never really the same product twice due to some customization, the overall effort was relatively comparable (e.g., an SAP implementation at one car company to the SAP implementation of another).

You see, all in all, while IT was somewhat different, there was enough similarity that practices borrowed from manufacturing worked. And they worked for a long time. But IT has changed a lot, and we haven't updated the way we manage it accordingly.

Using the factory analogy in IT conjures up images of people sitting in their cubicles and actioning work packages, with one person translating a requirement into a design, then handing it over to another person who writes a bit of code, then on to the next person who tests it—and in all of this, no one talks to each other. It's all done mechanically, as with people on an assembly line. (This is reminiscent of Charlie Chaplin in the movie *Modern Times*.) The world has changed, and a significant change enabler has entered the stage: the reduction in transaction, or setup, costs for IT.

The Concept of Transaction Costs and Batch Size Is Central for the Shift in Approach

Transaction costs (sometimes called setup costs) are the costs required to make a change in the production mechanism to either produce a different product or make changes to the way the same product is being produced. Transaction costs determine the optimal batch size of the product to achieve an economic outcome, as the holding costs are difficult to influence. How transaction costs influence the optimal batch size is illustrated in Figure 0.3.‡

The optimal batch size is determined by the holding costs and the transaction costs (higher holding costs drive smaller batch sizes and higher

---

‡ Stefan Thomke and Donald Reinertsen have probably written the best explanation of this in their May 2012 *Harvard Business Review* article, "Six Myths of Product Development." Although they talk about product development rather than IT explicitly, for all means and purposes, IT delivery is the delivery of an IT product.[1]

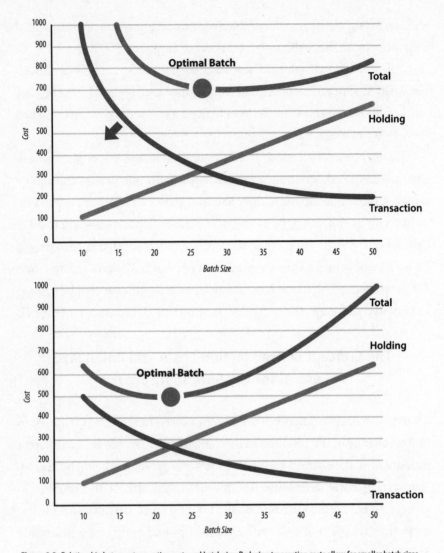

Figure 0.3: Relationship between transaction costs and batch size: Reducing transaction costs allow for smaller batch sizes

transaction costs drive larger batch sizes). In IT, the holding costs are a combination of the increasing cost of fixing a problem later in the life cycle and the missed benefit of features that are complete but not in production yet. These two factors don't change much with modern DevOps practices; what changes are the transaction costs.

As manufacturing has changed over the years, there has been a focus on reducing the transaction costs so that more differentiated products can be produced. This has cumulated in mass customization and 3-D printing. In IT, both Agile and DevOps have tried to achieve the same reductions.

In the past, the transaction costs were high for IT projects. You had to order hardware and install all the *middleware*, and the development of your customized software product included a lot of manual effort-intensive tasks, such as deploying code changes, regression testing the solution, making changes to the environments (for example, an MVP takes less than three months rather than 6–12 months; incremental releases take days/weeks instead of months).

This has changed now that the transaction costs have been significantly reduced by cloud-based infrastructure, anything as a service *(XaaS)*, and DevOps-inspired automation across the SDLC, which have made much smaller batch sizes possible.

And there is a real business benefit in small batch sizes. Small batch sizes allow us to invest smaller amounts to validate a business idea and make fewer large bets. The best analogy for this comes from long-time product developer Don Reinertsen:[2] Imagine a lottery where you get a prize if you guess a three-digit number correctly. One option is to give me five dollars and guess the three-digit number; I then tell you whether you have won the $1,000 prize. Alternatively, you can give me two dollars and guess the first digit. In return, I tell you the first digit of the winning number, and you can decide to pay another $2 for the next digit and again the same for the third digit. Would you choose the first game or the second game? I think it is clear that the second game provides you with a better outcome.[§] The feedback from the smaller batch

---

[§] Scenario 1: -3.995 = (-5×999/1000)+1/1000×1000. Scenario 2: -1.214 = (-2×9/10) + (4×1/10×9/10) + (-6×1/10×1/10×9/10) + 1000×1/10×1/10×1/10.

size provides you information to decide on further investment or not. This is exactly what customer feedback will allow you to do when you work on smaller increments of functionality and smaller batch sizes in your IT projects.

We also want smaller batches for a couple of other reasons. Smaller batch sizes reduce the complexity in IT delivery, as there is a smaller amount of changes to consider in testing and during *go-live*. In manufacturing, you can scale to larger batch sizes more easily, as you can run the same process for larger batches without the inherent complexity penalties that appear when trying to scale your IT solution. Smaller batch sizes in IT allow us to test the direction the product is developing, with customer feedback leveraged to direct the creative nature of IT products.[ll] In manufacturing, it is much more difficult to iteratively create and validate a product; just imagine building one product in a factory (e.g., a car), selling it, and then using feedback to build the next one, and so forth. The delays and costs would explode quickly. Eric Ries's Lean Startup method[3] has been adapted for physical goods by FastWorks with great results (reduced cost, increased speed),[4] but the preference for larger batch sizes will remain a feature of manufacturing (at least until 3-D printing of everything has become the norm and reduces the setup/transaction costs).[5]

With smaller batch sizes comes a very different economic model for governance to minimize the required overhead from management. In other words, the technical transaction cost has been reduced, but the management-related and architecture-related transaction costs have not been reduced at the same time. This is because we still follow the same ideas and principles that are inspired by manufacturing. With this book, I want to help you change this.

[ll] In IT, due to the trial-and-error nature of product-development work, smaller batches have the benefit of reduced risk and faster feedback. This is different from manufacturing, where efficiency and productivity are measurable.

In the appendix, I provide a closer look at some ideas and principles that have been adopted by IT from manufacturing and whether or not they are still applicable.

I hope this book will help you all to create IT delivery organizations that don't resemble Charlie Chaplin's *Modern Times* but are engaging workplaces where IT people work with business stakeholders to build meaningful solutions for customers. As my Accenture colleague Mark Rendell has said, "DevOps is not about making IT efficient. It's about making business effective through IT."[6]

Let's jump right in and get started with the transformation.

PART A

Creating the Right Ecosystem

In my role as a consultant, I have to explain to technology leaders frequently that knowledge of what good looks like and the best intentions unfortunately don't always result in the best outcome. The ecosystem that the company leadership creates plays a huge role in how successful a transformation can be. The ecosystem you are likely working in has been created within the context of your legacy—the things that have been in the past and the systems that were built previously.

The concept of legacy is not just tied to your technologies and applications. As was explained in the introduction, there is a legacy mind-set inspired by a command-and-control culture, which I am trying to change with this book. So, what does it take to define a roadmap to guide this shift? How do you find the right technologies to work with? And what makes a good partner who can join you on this journey away from legacy toward the new?

With the toolkit provided in part A of this book, you will be a significant step closer to creating an ecosystem that allows IT to thrive and transform. It describes the high-level considerations for creating an ecosystem that supports the transformation to a modern IT development organization. I will cover the transformation journey, multispeed IT, your application portfolio, working with legacy, choosing software packages, and finding the right delivery partners. I will also discuss how my team works together with our clients at the leadership level to explore how the ecosystem needs to change for the benefit of both organizations, I will provide some of that analysis toolkit with activities that you can run yourself. Together, this information will help you understand how to leverage your legacy as an enabler rather than as a hindrance.

CHAPTER 1

The Roadmap to Transformation

Alice asked the Cheshire Cat, who was sitting in a tree, "What road
do I take?" The cat asked, "Where do you want to go?" "I don't know,"
Alice answered. "Then," said the cat, "it really doesn't matter, does it?"
—**Lewis Carroll**, *Alice's Adventures in Wonderland*

Many challenges in your IT delivery process are caused by bottlenecks, which lengthen the time before you get meaningful feedback
that you can, in turn, use to improve your process and products. Making
work visible is one of the most powerful ways to identify bottlenecks, yet
IT is mostly dealing with invisible work: there is no visible stock showing
how much product a team or facility has created, there is no warehouse
that indicates how much product is available but not in use, and there
is no physical process that you can follow to see how an output is being
created from the inputs. This leads to an interesting situation: while most
people working in manufacturing have a rough idea of how their product
is being created, in IT, the actual process is a lot less known. And I mean
the real process, not the one that might be documented on some company
web page or in some methodology. Yet without that visibility it is difficult
to improve the process. So, one absolutely crucial task for any IT executive
is to make the process visible, including status and measures like quality
and speed. In this chapter, we leverage value stream maps to make work

visible and jump-start the transformation with an initial roadmap and governance approach.

Making the IT Process Visible

I like to start any DevOps consulting activity with a *value stream mapping exercise*. The reason is quite simple: it is the most reliable exercise to align everyone in the organization and my team to what the IT process looks like. You could look at the methodology page or some large Visio diagrams for the IT delivery process, but more often than not, reality has evolved away from those documented processes.

I have outlined the process to run such an exercise at the end of the chapter so that you can try this too. In short, you are bringing representatives from all parts of the organization together in a room to map out your current IT delivery process as it is being experienced by the people on the ground and, perhaps more importantly, reveals areas within the system that can be improved. I suggest that you engage an experienced facilitator or at least find someone unbiased to run the meeting for you.

Ideally, we want to be able to objectively measure the IT process in regard to throughput, *cycle time*, and quality. Unfortunately, this is often a work-intensive exercise. Running a value stream mapping exercise every three to six months (depending on how quickly you change and improve things) will give you a good way to keep progress on the radar while investing just a few hours each month. It will highlight your current process, the cycle time, and any quality concerns. You want to make the result of the exercise visible somewhere in your office, as that will help focus people on improving this process. It will act as a visible reminder that improving this process is important to the organization.

Once you have a good understanding of the high-level IT process and the areas that require improvement, you can then create a first roadmap for the transformation.

Creating a First Roadmap

Roadmaps are partly science and partly art. Many roadmaps look similar at the high level, yet on the more detailed level, no two people create the exact same roadmap. The good news is that there is no *one* right answer for roadmaps anyway. In true Agile fashion, it is most important to understand the direction and to have some milestones for evaluating progress and making IT visible. Many things will change over time, and you will need to manage this. There are a few guidelines on how to create a good roadmap for this transformation.

Based on the value stream map of your IT delivery process, you will be able to identify bottlenecks in the process. As *systems thinking*, *theory of constraints*, and *queuing theory* teach us, unless we improve one of the bottlenecks in the process, every other improvement will not lead to a faster outcome overall. This is important, as sometimes we spend our change energy on "shiny objects" rather than focusing on things that will make a real difference. One good way to identify bottlenecks is to use the value stream mapping exercise and let all stakeholders in the room vote on the problems that, if addressed, will make a real difference to overall IT delivery. The wisdom of the crowd in most cases does identify a set of bottlenecks that are worth addressing.

There are two other considerations for your roadmap to be a success: flow and speed of delivery rather than cost and quality. A focus on flow is the ultimate systems thinking device to break down silos in your organization. In the past, the "owner" of a function, like the testing center of excellence or the development factory, ran improvement initiatives to make its area of influence and control more effective. Over time, this created highly optimized functions for larger batch sizes to the detriment of the overall flow of delivery. Flow improves with small batch sizes.

There are usually three ways to evaluate IT delivery: speed, cost, and quality. Traditionally, we focused our improvements on cost or quality, which, in turn, often reduced the speed of delivery. If you evaluate your IT delivery by just looking to improve quality, you often introduce additional quality gates, which cost you more and take longer to adhere to. If you evaluate your IT function based on reduced cost, the most common approaches are to push more work to less experienced people or to skip steps in the process, which often leads to lower quality and lower speed due to rework. Focusing on cost or quality without considering the impact on flow is therefore an antipattern for successful IT in my experience.

In contrast, focusing on speed, specifically on bottlenecks that prevent fast delivery of really small batches, will bring the focus back to the overall flow of delivery and hence improve speed of delivery in general (even for larger batches), leading to improvements in quality and cost over time. It is impossible to achieve higher speed if the quality is bad, as the required rework will ultimately slow you down. The only way to really improve speed is to automate and remove unnecessary steps in the process. Just typing faster is unlikely to do much for the overall speed. So, speed is the ultimate forcing function for IT. I have been in transformations with clients where cost was reduced but the overall delivery experience continued to be bad for business stakeholders. I have also seen a lot of quality improvement initiatives that stifled IT delivery and nearly ground it to a halt. I have yet to see the same problem with improvement initiatives that evaluate based on speed.

Two words of caution when it comes to speed: The first one is really not that bad of a problem. You can obviously "game" the speed evaluation criteria by breaking work down further and delivering smaller batches, which can be delivered faster. While this does not result in a like-for-like comparison of the speed between batches, it is still a win for the organization, as smaller batches are less risky. The second warning is that people might look for shortcuts that increase risk or reduce quality. To prevent this, you need to continue to look for quality measures on top of speed to make sure that quality is not dropping as speed increases. To evaluate for speed, you will look at work coming through your delivery life cycle, and the process of measuring it will make it more visible to you. Good measures for speed are cycle time for work items (cycle time = time from work item approved to work item completed and available in production) or volume of work delivered per time period.

As Figure 1.1 demonstrates, your overall transformation roadmap will likely have milestones focused on different functions and capabilities (e.g., automated regression testing available, lightweight business case introduced), which makes sense. However, there is another dimension, which is the coverage of applications and technologies. In the next chapter, I will explain how to do an application portfolio analysis that allows you to identify sets of applications that you uplift as part of the transformation. Your roadmap should include prioritized sets (often called waves) of applications, as any organization at scale will not be able to uplift absolutely everything. You shouldn't anyway, as some applications might not be worth the effort and cost of an uplift.

One last comment on the transformation roadmap: many capabilities and changes require a significant amount of time to implement. Unfortunately, organizations are not very patient with change programs, so you need to make sure that you build in some early and visible wins. For those early and visible wins, all other rules do not apply. They can be with applications that are not critical for the business or in areas that are not part of a bottleneck. The goal of those wins is to keep the momentum and allow the organization to see progress. You should see these as being part of the change-management activities of the transformation. Of course, ideally, the early and visible wins are also in one of the priority areas identified earlier.

Transforming your IT organization will take time. In Figure 1.2, you can see a transformation blueprint that is common among clients I work with. The pattern shown here is something I have seen again and again. It starts with adopting Agile and then realizing that Agile without DevOps practices (like test automation, deployment automation, etc.) does not allow you to speed up as much as you were hoping for. As you adopt DevOps and become faster, you start to realize the organizational bound-

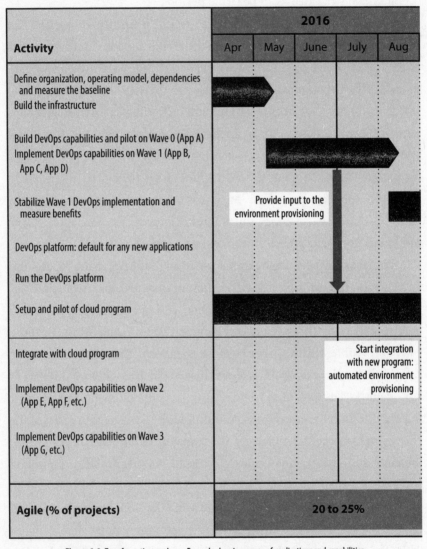

Figure 1.1: Transformation roadmap: Example showing waves of applications and capabilities

aries and speed bumps that are embedded in the operating model, which require some real organizational muscle and executive support to address. Don't be discouraged if things don't change overnight.

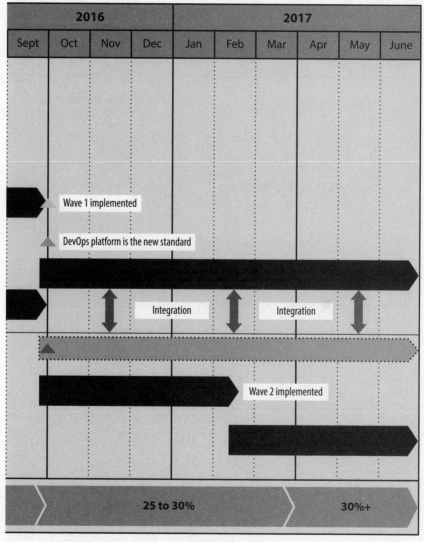

Figure 1.1, cont.

Governing the Transformation

As mentioned earlier, the roadmap is important, but without appropriate transformation governance, it is not going to get you much success. All too often, transformations get stuck. It is not possible to foresee all the

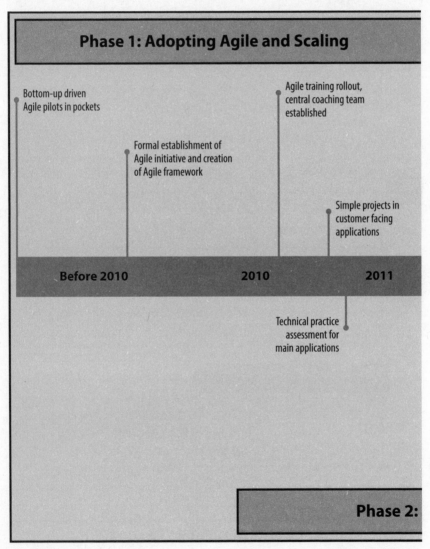

Figure 1.2: Common transformation blueprint: Changing your organization takes time as you adopt different methods

challenges that will hinder progress, and without appropriate governance that finds the right balance between discipline and flexibility, the transformation will stall. Transformation governance makes the progress of the transformation visible and allows you to steer it. It's different from the normal IT delivery governance that you run for your delivery initiatives (e.g.,

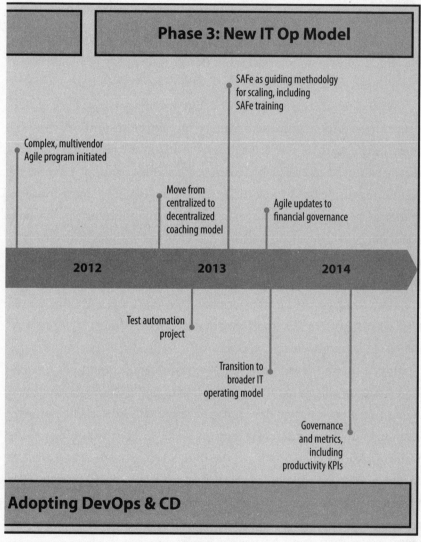

Figure 1.2, cont.

change review boards). In a meeting with a number of transformation change agents and consultants at the 2015 DevOps Enterprise Summit, we tried to identify what it takes to be successful when adopting DevOps. We all had different ideas and were working in different organizations, but we could agree on one thing that we believed was the characteristic of a successful organization: the ability to continuously improve and manage the continuous improvement process.

This continuous improvement and the adaption of the roadmap are the largest contributors to success in transforming your IT organization. DevOps and Agile are not goals; hence, there is no target state as such.

What does successful transformation governance look like? Governance covers a lot of areas, so it is important that you know what you are comparing against as you make progress with your transformation. This means you need to establish a baseline for the measures of success that you decide on before you start the transformation. Too many transformations I have seen spent six months improving the situation but then could not provide evidence of what had changed beyond anecdotes such as "but we have continuous integration with *Jenkins* now." Unfortunately, this does not necessarily convince business or other IT stakeholders to continue to invest in the transformation. In one case, even though the CIO was supportive, the transformation lost funding due to a lack of evidence of the improvements.

If you can, however, prove that by introducing continuous integration you were able to reduce the instances of build-related environment outages by 30%, now you have a great story to tell. As a result, I strongly recommend running a baselining exercise in the beginning of the transformation. Think about all the things you care about and want to measure along the way, and identify the right way to baseline them. (I've provided some examples in Table 1.1.) I will talk a bit more about how to measure metrics when we talk about delivery governance later in this chapter.

Metric	Definition	Measurement
Release Cycle Time	The average time it takes to approve a work package (user story, feature, set of requirements) and release it	Usually measured as the time difference between work item states in your work tracking system
Cost of Release	The effort it takes to release new functionality, measured as effort for all release activities performed for go-live (a variation of this only counts effort outside of business hours)	Typically based on timesheets
Regression Duration	Time it takes to validate that a change has not caused regression	The time between deployment and the "all clear" from either an automated or manual validation
Production Availability	Percentage production is available to perform the right service	Measured by a percentage of time production is functionally available or percentage of successful transactions
Mean time to Recovery	Time it takes to rectify any production issue	Measured from time of occurrence until full user functionality is achieved
Longevity of Teams	The average duration teams stay together	Measured as months before teams get disbanded and restructured for new projects

Table 1.1: Baseline metrics: These metrics have proven to be successful in guiding transformations

The other important aspect of transformation governance is creating flexibility and accountability. For each improvement initiative, as part of the roadmap, you want to leverage the scientific method:

- Formulate a hypothesis, including a measure of success.
- Baseline the measure.
- Once the implementation is complete, evaluate the result against the hypothesis.

Some things will work, some won't; and during governance, you want to learn from both. Don't blame the project team for a failed hypothesis (after all, it should have been we, as leaders, who originally approved the investment—so, who is really to blame?). You should only provide negative feedback where the process has not been followed (e.g., measures were not in place or results were "massaged"), which prevents you from learning.

As you learn, the next set of viable improvement initiatives will change. Your evaluation criteria of the initiatives you want to start next should be guided by:

- previous learnings,
- the size of the initiative following a *weighted shortest job first* (WSJF) approach,
- and how well the team can explain the justification for the initiative.

Don't allow yourself to be tempted by large business cases that require a lot of up-front investments; rather, ask for smaller initial steps to validate the idea before investing heavily. You should keep an eye on the overall roadmap over time to see that the milestones are achievable. If they are not anymore, you can either change the amount of improvement initiatives or, when unavoidable, update the roadmap.

In the transformation governance process, you want representation of all parts of the organization to make sure the change is not biased to a specific function (e.g., test, development, operations). Governance meetings should be at least once a month and should require as little documentation as possible. Having the transformation team spend a lot of time on elaborate PowerPoint presentations for each meeting is not going to help your transformation. Ideally, you will look at real-time data, your value stream map, and lightweight business cases for the improvement ideas.

Making IT Delivery Visible

Talking about making things visible and using real data, it should be clear that some of the DevOps capabilities can be extremely useful for this. One of the best visual aids in your toolkit is the deployment pipeline.* A deployment pipeline is a visual representation of the process that software follows from the developer to production, with all the stages in between. This visual representation shows what is happening to the software as well as any positive or negative results of it. I have provided an example in Figure 1.3 from one of the solutions that I often work with. You can see how the different stages of the life cycle and the associated activities are represented in the pipeline view.[1] This deployment pipeline provides direct insights into the quality of your software in real time. You might choose to provide additional information in a *dashboard* as an aggregate or to enrich the core data with additional information, but the deployment pipeline provides the core backbone. It also creates a forcing function, as all the steps are represented and enforced, and the results can be seen directly from the dashboard, which reduces the chance of people doing

---

* Gary Gruver wrote a whole book, *Starting and Scaling DevOps in the Enterprise*, about the deployment pipeline as a means to drive the transformation.

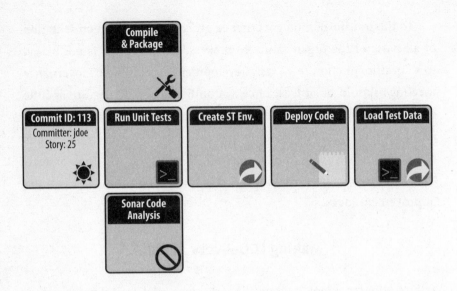

Figure 1.3: Deployment pipeline example: Accenture DevOps platform provides a look into the deployment process

things that are not visible. Any improvements and process changes will be visible in the deployment pipeline as long as it remains the only allowed way to deliver changes. Where you don't have easy access to metrics you can also add steps to each stage to log out metrics for later consumption in your analytics solution.

Having an analytics solution in your company to create real-time dashboards is important. Most companies these days either use a commercial visualization or analytics solution or build something based on the many *open source* options (like Graphite). The key here is to use the data that is being created all through the SDLC to create meaningful dashboards that can then be leveraged not only during the transformation governance but at any other point in time. High-performing teams have connected their DevOps tool chain with analytics dashboards and

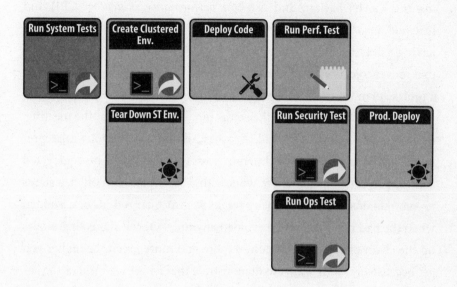

Figure 1.3, cont.

it allows us to see important information in real time. For example, we can see how good the quality of a release is, how the quality of the release package relates to post-deployment issues, and how much test automation has improved our defect rate in later phases of the SDLC.

Governing IT Delivery

IT governance is, in my view, one of the undervalued elements in the transformation journey. Truth be told, most governance approaches are pretty poor and achieve very little of the outcome they are intended to achieve. Most governance meetings I have observed or been part of are based on red/amber/green status reports, which are subjective in nature and are not a good way of representing status. Furthermore, while the criteria for the color scheme might be defined somewhere, it often comes down to the leadership looking the project manager in the eyes and asking what she really thinks. Project managers from a *Project Management Institute* (*PMI*) background use *cost performance indicator* (CPI) and *schedule performance indicator* (SPI), which are slightly better but rely on having a detailed and appropriate project plan to report against. I argue that most projects evolve over time, which means that if you're preparing a precise plan for the whole project, you plan to be precisely wrong.[†]

Additionally, by the time the status report is presented at the meeting, it is—at best—a few hours old. At worst, it's an unconscious misrepresentation, because so many different messages needed to be aggregated and the project manager had to work with poor inputs. Too often, a status report remains green over many weeks just to turn red all of a sudden when the bad news cannot be avoided anymore. Or the status that moves up the chain of command becomes more and more green the higher you get because everyone wants to demonstrate that he is in control of the situation. Remember, one of our goals with status reports is to make IT work visible, and we're not doing that in a meaningful way if the information we're presenting isn't a factual representation of our processes and progress.

What you should use in your governance of delivery are objective measures, such as number of working features, time to recover from an incident, cycle time for features to be delivered, and stories/features delivered and accepted per iteration. Those provide more meaningful ways to evaluate progress and quality. This information as well as other metrics should not be manually collected; you should be able to get the information from a real-time system or dashboard. Some metrics can be taken from your delivery pipeline, but many require additional data points from other systems (e.g., your Agile life-cycle-management tool). The "color commentary" is provided by the project team, and it can

---

[†] Inspired by Carveth Read: "It is better to be vaguely right than exactly wrong."[2]

either be overlayed as a discussion thread or annotated snapshots can be created for your governance meeting (see the example of an annotated burnup in Figure 1.4).

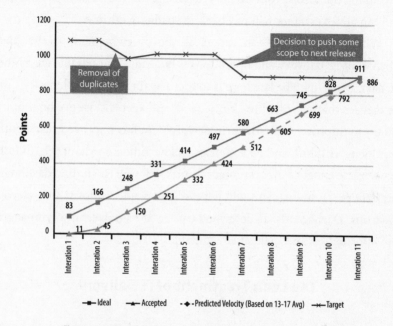

Figure 1.4: Annotated burnup chart: Burnup charts provide an annotated status of the project

The same is true for the metrics that you use during delivery governance. There is really no excuse for not having all the data available for each stage of your IT delivery process. It surprises me that we use IT to build great analytics solutions for our businesses, yet we don't utilize the same powerful solutions within IT to improve our area of the organization. Manual gathering of metrics is not acceptable when it is so easy to build steps into your process that automatically log the data. In the very worst case, you build a little bit of automation for each step that dumps the data out into a common logging format. I've had to do this many times, as most tools used during the SDLC do not expose the captured data in ways that they can easily be consumed. Rather, most tools assume that you can rely on the built-in reporting functionality, which often is not the case. You want to be able to relate data from one tool to another (and probably across tool vendors), so you will have to do some custom tooling to make sure all the data from your SDLC is available for your analysis. This relatively small investment will pay back in spades over time.

With all this data, you can easily be overwhelmed, as the "data exhaust" of IT delivery and operations is huge and comparable with other big data scenarios. The key here is to focus again on the bottlenecks. Find the metrics that represent the bottlenecks and keep a close eye on them as you try to improve. Once the primary problem has improved sufficiently, your focus will shift, and new metrics will become important. Thankfully, if you create a metric measurement framework well (including dashboard and data preparation), you will have all the needed information at your fingertips. Dashboards, as described earlier, are a powerful way to aggregate information and make it consumable.

The Lean Treatment of IT Delivery

In transformations, our focus is often on technologies and technical practices, yet a lot can be improved by applying Lean to IT delivery governance. By IT delivery governance, I mean any step of the overall IT delivery process where someone has to approve something before it can proceed. This can be project-funding checkpoints, deployment approvals for test environments, change control boards, and so on. During the SDLC there are usually many such governance steps for approvals or reviews, which all consume time and effort. And governance processes often grow over time. After a problem has occurred, we do a post-implementation review and add another governance step to prevent the same problem from happening again. After all, it can't hurt to be extra sure by checking twice. Over time, this creates a bloated governance process with steps that do not add value and diffuse accountability. I have seen deployment approval processes that required significantly more time than the actual deployment without adding value or improving quality. I find that some approval steps are purely administrative and have, over time, evolved to lose their meaning as the information is not really evaluated as it was intended. The following analysis will help you unbloat the process.

I want you to take a good, hard look at each step in your governance process to understand (a) how often a step actually makes an impact (e.g., an approval is rejected), (b) what the risk is of not doing it, and (c) what the cost is of performing this step.

Let's look at each of the three aspects in more detail:

1. When you look at approvals and review steps during the SDLC, how often are approvals not given or how often did reviews find issues that had to be addressed? (And I mean serious issues, not just rejections due to formalities such as using the wrong format of the review form.) The less often the process actually yields meaningful outcomes, the more likely it is that the process is not adding a lot of value. The same is true if approvals are in the high ninetieth percentile. Perhaps a notification is sufficient rather than waiting for the approval, which is extremely likely to come anyway. Or perhaps you can cut this step completely. I worked with one client whose deployment team had to chase approvals for pretty much every deployment after all the preparation steps were complete, adding hours or sometimes days to the deployment *lead time*. The approver was not actually doing a meaningful review, which we could see from the little time it took to approve once the team followed up with the approver directly. It was clearly just a rubber-stamping exercise. I recommended removing this approval and changing the process to send information to the approver before and after the deployment, including the test results. Lead time was significantely reduced, the approver

had less work, and because a manual step was removed, we could automate the deployment process end to end.

2. If we went ahead without the approval or review step and something went wrong, how large is the risk? How long would it take us to find out we have a problem and correct it by either fixing it or withdrawing the change? If the risk is low, then, again, the governance step might best be skipped or changed to a notification only.

3. What is the actual cost of the governance step in both effort and time? How long does it take to create the documentation for this step? How much time does each stakeholder involved spend on it? How much of the cycle time is being consumed while waiting for approvals to proceed?

With this information, you can calculate whether or not the governance step should continue to be used or whether you are better off abandoning or changing it. From my experience, about half the review and approval steps can either be automated (as the human stakeholder is following simple rules) or changed to a notification only, which does not prevent the process from progressing. I challenge you to try this in your organization and see how many things you can remove or automate, getting as close as possible to the minimum viable governance process. I have added an exercise for this at the end of the chapter.

First Steps for Your Organization

There are three exercises that I find immensely powerful because they achieve a significant amount of benefit for very little cost: (1) value stream mapping of your IT delivery process, (2) baselining your metrics, and (3) reviewing your IT governance. With very little effort, you can get a much better insight into your IT process and start making improvements.

Value Stream Mapping of Your IT Delivery Process

While there is a formal process for how to do value stream mapping, I will provide you with a smaller-scale version that, in my experience, works reasonably well for the purpose that we are after: making the process visible and improving some of the bottlenecks.[‡] Here is my shortcut version of value stream mapping:

1. Get stakeholders from all key parts of the IT delivery supply chain into a room (e.g., business stakeholders, development, testing, project management office (PMO), operations, business analysis).
2. Prepare a whiteboard with a high-level process for delivery. Perhaps write "business idea," "business case," "project kickoff," "development," "testing/QA," "deployment/release," and "value creation" on the board to provide some guidance.
3. Ask everyone in the room to write steps of the IT process on index cards for fifteen minutes. Next, ask them to post these cards on the whiteboard and work as a group to represent a complete picture of the IT delivery process on the whiteboard. Warning: you might have to encourage people to stand up and work together, or you may need to step in when/if discussions get out of hand.
4. Once the process is mapped, ask one or more people to walk the group through the overall process, and ask everyone to call out if anything is missing.

[‡] It is worthwhile for you to pick up *Value Stream Mapping* by Karen Martin and Mike Osterling if you want to formalize this process further.

5. Now that you have a reasonable representation of the process, you can do some deep dives to understand cycle times of the process, hot spots of concerns for stakeholders due to quality or other aspects, and tooling that supports the process.

6. Get people to vote on the most important bottleneck (e.g., give each person three votes to put on the board by putting a dot next to the process step).

In my experience, this exercise is the best way to make your IT delivery process visible. You can redo this process every three to six months to evaluate whether you addressed the key bottleneck and to see how the process has evolved. You can make the outcome of this process visible somewhere in your office to show the improvement priorities for each person/team involved. The highlighted bottlenecks will provide you with the checkpoints for your initial roadmap, as those are the things that your initiatives should address.

Baselining Your Metrics

Because having a baseline of your metrics is such an important part of the transformation governance, I want you to spend a few minutes filling out your own Table 1.2. Identify the metrics you care about now and in the future, and identify the mechanism you will use to baseline them. There are a couple of ways to identify the baseline. The baseline approach can be based on surveys, time-in-motion studies, or, ideally, existing and historical data. Where this is not possible, you should think about investing in an automated way to measure this metric. Where that fails, you can run a manual investigation and measuring process (e.g., time-in-motion studies), but those are less reliable and more time consuming.

Metric	Definition	Measurement Mechanism	Baseline Approach	Baseline Value
Release cycle time	The average time it takes for a story to go from a "ready" state to being deployed in production	Extract of date and time from Agile life-cycle-management system	Historical analysis of the last six months of user stories that were successfully deployed in production	168 days

Table 1.2: Metrics definitions example: Metrics should have definitions, measuring mechanisms, and baseline values

Reviewing Your IT Governance Process

There is a lot of talk about automation to help improve the IT delivery process when it comes to speed of delivery and quality. One thing that people underestimate is how much they can influence by just improving their governance process. Here is a short checklist that you can use to review your governance process. Ask these questions to guide where IT delivery governance is really required. Based on the answers, you can evaluate the impact and risk of removing the process step, ideally even with an economic model reflecting monetary impact and risk probability.

IT governance checklist:

- How often has someone rejected a submission to the checkpoint based on reasons other than process compliance?
- What would really happen to the process if an incorrect decision was made?
- What value is being added by the person approving this checkpoint that a computer could not provide automatically based on a number of inputs?

- How much time and money are being spent on this governance process (including the usual wait time that initiatives encounter while waiting for approvals)?
- Is this governance step based on objective measures or a subjective measure? How do you know?

CHAPTER 2

Accepting the Multispeed Reality (for Now)

> If everything is important, then nothing is.
>
> **—Anonymous**

Clients I work with often have a thousand or more applications in their portfolio. Clearly, we cannot make changes to all of them at the same time. This chapter looks at how to navigate the desire for innovative new systems and the existing web of legacy applications. We will identify *minimum viable clusters* of applications to start your transformation and perform an application portfolio analysis to support this.

One of the trends in the industry that has caused the increase in interest in Agile and DevOps practices was the arrival of internet natives, as I mentioned in the introduction. Those companies have the advantage that their applications are newer than most applications are in a large-enterprise context. "Legacy" is often used as a derogatory term in the industry, but the reality is that any code in production is really legacy already. And any new code we are writing today will be legacy tomorrow. Trying to differentiate between legacy and nonlegacy is a nearly impossible task over time.

In the past, organizations tried to deal with legacy through transformation projects that took many years and tried to replace older legacy systems with new systems. Yet very often, many old systems survived for one reason or another, and the overall application architecture became more complicated. These big-bang transformations are not the way things are done anymore, as the speed of evolution requires organizations to be adaptable while they are changing their IT architecture.

I think we all can agree that what we want is really fast, flexible, and reliable IT delivery. So, should we throw away our "legacy" applications and build a new set of "fast applications"? I think reality is more nuanced. I have worked with dozens of organizations that are struggling with the tension between fast digital applications and slow enterprise applications. Some of these organzations just came off a large transformation that was trying to solve this problem, but at the end of the multiyear transformation, the new applications were already slow-legacy again. A new approach is required that is more practical and more maintainable, and still achieves the outcome.

While we want everything to be fast, we have to accept that the architecture of some applications and the years of accrued *technical debt** might not allow every application to be delivered at the same speed. There are discussions about *bimodal IT* (using two methods of delivery, such as Waterfall for predictability and Agile for exploration)[1] or *multimodal IT* (using several different methods, such as several Agile and Waterfall flavors), which classify applications by type (*systems of engagement* for customer interaction and *systems of record* for internal

---

* I speak about technical debt quite a bit in this chapter, so I wanted to leave you with a few thoughts on how to measure it. There are, of course, the static code-analysis tools that provide a view of technical debt based on coding issues. I think that is a good starting point. I would add to this the cost to deploy the application (e.g., how many hours of people does it require to deploy into a test or production environment), the cost of regression testing the product (how many hours or people time does it take to validate nothing has broken), and the cost of creating a new environment with the application. If you are more ambitious, you can also look for measures of complexity and dependencies with other applications, but I have not yet seen a good repeatable way for measuring those. The first four I mention are relatively easy to determine and should therefore be the basis for your measure of technical debt.

facing processes).[2] I think this hard classification is somewhat danger-ous when it comes to speed; if your core business relies on systems of record to differentiate yourself, then those should be delivered as fast and as reliably as possible. Many organizations use the classification as an excuse to not improve some applications, which is wrong from a business-value perspective.

In the rest of the chapter, I will propose an alternative method that I use with my clients to help shape a multispeed approach with the ultimate goal of everything being as fast as is feasible and economically sensible, which might mean one or more different delivery speeds in the future.

Analyzing Your Application Portfolio

Large organizations often have hundreds if not thousands of applications, so it would be unrealistic to assume that we can uplift all applications at the same time. Some applications probably don't need to be uplifted, as they don't change often or are not of strategic importance. In the exercise section of this chapter, I provide details so that you can run your own analysis.

With this analysis, we can do a couple of things: we can prioritize applications into clusters (I will talk about that a little bit more later) and gather the applications into three different groupings that will determine how we will deal with each application as we are transforming IT delivery. The groupings will determine how you will invest and how you will work with the software vendors and your delivery partners.

The first group is for applications that we want to divest from or keep steady at a low volume of change. Let's call this *true legacy* to dif-ferentiate it from the word "legacy," which is often used just for older systems. In the true legacy category, you will sort applications that are hardly ever changing, that are not supporting business-critical processes, and in which you are not investing. I think it is pretty obvious that you don't want to spend much money automating the delivery life cycle for these applications. For these applications, you will likely not spend much time with the software vendor of the application, and you will choose a low-cost delivery partner that "keeps the lights on" if you don't want to deal with them in-house. And you really shouldn't invest your IT skills in these applications.

The second group is for applications that are supporting your business but are a little bit removed from your customers. Think of ERP or HCM systems—these are the "workhorses" for your applications. You spend a bulk of your money on running and updating these systems, and they are likely the ones that determine your overall speed of delivery for larger projects. Improving workhorses will allow you to deliver projects faster and more reliably, but the technologies of many of these workhorses are not as easily adaptable to DevOps and Agile practices. It is crucial to these systems that you work closely with the software vendor to make the technology more DevOps suitable (I will talk about that in the next chapter). If you choose to get help maintaining and evolving these systems, make sure the partner you work with understands your need to evolve the way of working as well as the system itself.

The third group are your "innovation engines" applications. These are the customer-facing applications that you can use to drive innovation or, on the flip side, that can cause you a lot of grief if customers don't like what you are presenting to them. The challenge here is that most of these will rely on the workhorses to deliver the right experience. My favorite example is the banking mobile app, which you can experiment with but only in so far as it continues to show accurate information about your bank accounts; otherwise, you will get very upset as a customer. Here, you will likely use custom technologies. You should work very closely with your software vendor if you chose a *commercial-off-the-shelf* (COTS) *product*, and the delivery partner should be a co-creator, not just a delivery partner.

Now this grouping of applications is not static. As your application architecture evolves, certain applications will move between groups;

that means your vendor and delivery-partner strategy evolves with it. Active application portfolio management is becoming increasingly more important as the speed of evolution increases and application architectures become more modular. Continuing with the chapter 1 theme of making things visible, the best way to represent the analysis is by using an application radar, which has "innovation engines" in the middle and true legacy on the outside.

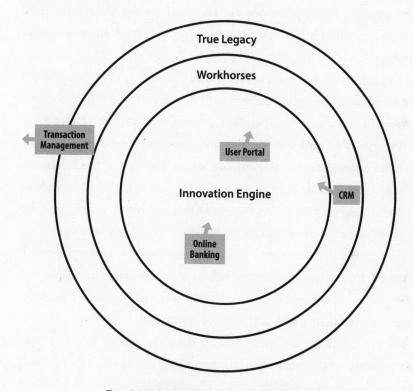

Figure 2.1: Application radar: Makes the status of each application visible

Finding a Minimum Viable Cluster

The Agile principle of small batch sizes applies for transformations as well. We can use the information from the application portfolio analysis above to guide us. It is very likely that the categories of workhorses and innovation engines contain too many applications to work on at the same time. Rather than just picking the first x applications, you need to do a bit more analysis to find what I call a minimum viable cluster.

Applications don't exist in isolation from each other. This means that most functional changes to your application landscape will require you to update more than one application. This, in turn, means that even if you are able to speed up one application, you might not be able to actually speed up delivery, as you will continue to wait on the other applications to deliver their changes.

The analogy of the weakest link comes to mind; in this case, it is the slowest link that determines your overall delivery speed. What you need to determine is the minimum viable cluster of applications. The best way of doing this is to rank your application based on several factors, such as customer centricity and volume of change. The idea of the minimum viable cluster is that you incrementally review your highest-priority application and analyze the dependencies of that application. You look for a small subset of those applications in which you can see a significant improvement of delivery speed when you improve the delivery speed of this subset. (Sometimes you might still have to deal with further dependencies, but in most cases, the subset should allow you to make significant changes independently with a little bit of creativity.)

You can continue the analysis for further clusters so that you have some visibility of the next applications you will start to address. Don't spend too much time clustering all applications. As you make progress, you can do rolling-wave identification of the clusters.

I want to mention a few other considerations when thinking about the prioritization of applications. First, I think it is important that you start to work on meaningful applications as early as possible. Many organizations experiment with new automation techniques on isolated applications with no serious business impact. Many techniques that work for those

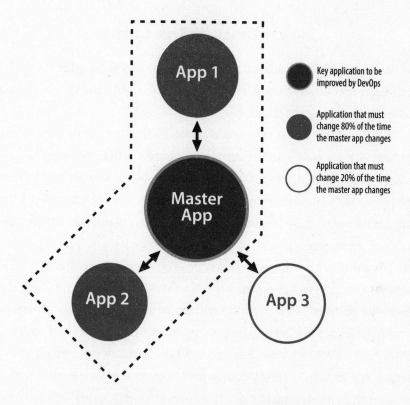

Figure 2.2: Minimum viable cluster: Applies system thinking to application analysis

applications might not scale to the rest of the IT landscape, and the rest of the organization might not identify with the change for that application. ("This does not work for our real systems" is a comment you might hear in this context.)

Because the uplift of your minimum viable cluster can take a while, it might make sense to find "easier" pilots to (a) provide some early wins and (b) allow you to learn techniques that are more advanced before you need to adapt them for your first minimum viable cluster. The key to this is making sure that considerations from the minimum viable cluster are being proven with the simpler application so that the relevance is clear to the organization. Collaboration across the different application stakeholders is critical to achieving this.

How to Deal with True Legacy

We have spoken about the strategy that you should employ for the applications that continue to be part of your portfolio, but what should you do with the true legacy applications?

Obviously, the best thing to do would be to get rid of them completely. Ask yourself whether the functionality is still truly required. Too often, we hang on to systems for small pieces of functionality that cannot be replicated somewhere else, because the hidden cost of maintaining the application is not visible; not enough effort is being put into decommissioning the system.

Assuming this is not an option, we should use for architecture what software engineers have been using in their code for a long time, the *strangler pattern*.[3] The strangler pattern in this case means we try to erode the legacy application by moving functions to our newer applications bit by bit. Over time, less and less functionality will remain in the legacy application until my earlier point comes true: the cost of maintaining the application just for the leftover functionality will become too high, and this will serve as the forcing function to finally decommission it.

The last trick in your "dealing with legacy" box is to make the real cost of the legacy application visible. The factors that should play into this cost are as follows:

- the delay other applications are encountering due to the legacy application,
- the defects caused by the legacy application,
- the amount of money spent maintaining and running the legacy application, and
- the opportunity cost of things you cannot do because of the legacy application being in place.

The more you are able to put a monetary number on this, the better your chances are to overcome the legacy complication over time by convincing the organization to do something about it.

I said before that every application you build now will be the legacy of tomorrow. At the increasing speed of IT development, this statement should make us nervous, as we are creating more and more legacy ever faster. This means that, ultimately, the best way to deal with legacy is to build our new legacy with the right mind-set. There is no *end-state architecture* anymore (well, there never was, as we now know—in spite of what enterprise architects kept telling us). As a result of this new architecture mind-set, each application should be built so that it can easily be decommissioned and to minimize its dependency on other applications. I will cover this in more detail in chapter 10.

Governing the Portfolio and Checkpoints

Your application portfolio is always evolving, and the only way to be successful in such a moving environment is to have the right governance in place. Governance was hard in the past; in the new world, it has become even more difficult. There are more things to govern, the overall speed of the delivery of changes has increased, and without a change in governance, governance will either slow down delivery or become overly expensive.

There are four main points of governance for any change:

- Checkpoint 1 (CP1): this answers the question of whether or not the idea we have for the change is good enough to deserve some funding to explore the idea further and come up with possible solutions.
- Checkpoint 2 (CP2): this answers the question of whether we have found a possible solution that is good enough to attempt as a first experiment or first release to validate our idea.

- Checkpoint 3 (CP3): this answers the question of whether or not the implemented solution has reached the right quality to be released to at least a small subaudience in production.
- Checkpoint 4 (CP4): this answers the question of whether or not the experiment was successful and what we will do next.

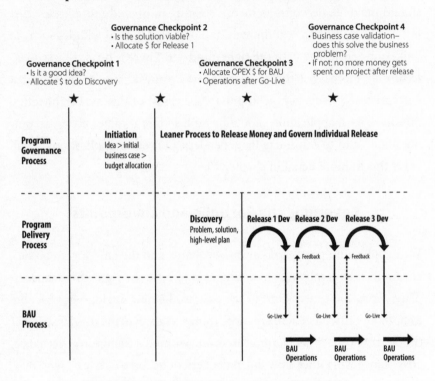

Figure 2.3: Governance checkpoints: An Agile governance process with four checkpoints

Checkpoint 1 (CP1)

At CP1, we are mostly talking about our business stakeholders. Somewhere in the organization, a good idea has come up or a problem has been found that requires fixing. Before we start spending money, our first checkpoint is to validate that we are exploring the right problems and opportunities that have a business impact, are of strategic importance, or are our "exploratory ideas" to find new areas of business. This checkpoint is a gatekeeper to make sure we are not starting too many new things at the same time and to focus our energy on the most promising ideas.

Between CP1 and CP2, the organization explores the idea, and both business and IT come together to run a *discovery* workshop that can take a couple of hours or multiple weeks depending on the scale of the problem. You can run this for a whole business transformation or for a small change. The goal of discovery really falls into three important areas: (1) everyone understands the problem and idea, (2) we explore what can be done with support of IT, and (3) we explore what the implementation could look like in regard to schedule and teams. This discovery session is crucial to enable your people to achieve the best outcome.

Checkpoint 2 (CP2)

After discovery, the next checkpoint is validation that we now have discovered something that is worth implementing. At this stage, we should check that we have capacity to support the implementation with all parties: IT, business stakeholders, the operations team, security, and anyone else impacted. This is a crucial checkpoint at which to embed architectural requirements, as it becomes more difficult to add them later on. Too often, business initiatives are implemented without due consideration of architectural aspects, which leads to increased technical debt over time.

It is my view that every initiative that is being supported by the organization with scarce resources such as money and people should leave the organization in a better place in two ways: it better supports the business, and it leaves the IT landscape better than it was before. This is the only reasonable way to reduce technical debt over time and deal with legacy. CP2 is the perfect time to make sure that the improvement of the IT landscape / down payment of technical debt is part of the project before it continues on to implementation. This has to be something that is not optional; otherwise, the slippery slope will lead back to the original state. It is quite easy to let the necessary rigor be lost when "just this once" we only need to quickly put this one temporary solution in place. I learned over the years that there is nothing more permanent than a temporary solution.

Between CP2 and CP3 is the bulk of the usual software delivery that includes design, development, and testing work being done in an Agile fashion. I am confident that Agile is the only methodology we will need going forward but that we will have different levels of rigor and speed as part of our day-to-day Agile delivery. Once the solution has matured over several iterations to being a release candidate, we will have CP3.

Checkpoint 3 (CP3)

At CP3, we will confirm that the release candidate has reached the right quality for us to release it to production. We will validate that the architecture considerations have been adhered to and technical debt has been paid down as agreed, and we will not introduce new technical debt unknowingly. (Sometimes we might consciously choose to accrue a little more debt to test something early but commit to fixing it in the next release. This should be a rare occasion, though.) This checkpoint is often associated with the change control board, which has to review and approve any changes to production. Of course, we are looking for the minimum viable governance here, and you can refer to the previous chapter for more details on general governance principles to follow at CP3.

Between CP3 and CP4 the product is in production and is being used. If we follow a proper Agile process, the team will already be working on the implementation of the next release in tandem with supporting the version that has just gone live. Internal or external stakeholders are using the product, and we gather feedback directly from the systems (through monitoring, analytics, and other means) or directly from the stakeholders by leveraging surveys, feedback forms, or any other communication channel.

Checkpoint 4 (CP4)

Checkpoint 4 is the checkpoint that is extremely underutilized in my experience. It's one of those processes that everyone agrees is important, yet very few have the rigor and discipline to really leverage it to meet its full potential. This checkpoint serves to validate that our idea and the solution approach are valid. Because projects are temporary by definition, the project team has often stood down already and team members have been allocated to other projects. CP4 then becomes a *pro forma* exercise that people don't appreciate fully. If we have persistent, long-lasting product teams, the idea of learning from the previous release and understanding the reaction of stakeholders is a lot more important. Those product teams are the real audience of CP4, though, of course, the organizational stakeholders are the other audience that needs to understand whether the money was well invested and whether further investment should be made.

CP4 should be an event for learning and a possibility for celebrating success; it should never be a negative experience. If the idea did not work out, we learned something useful about our product that we have to do differently next time. You can combine CP4 with a post-implementation review to look at the way the release was delivered and to improve the process as well as the product. It is my personal preference to run the post-implementation review separately to keep improving the product and the delivery process as two distinct activities.

With this governance model and the four checkpoints in place, you can manage delivery in several speeds and deal with the faster pace. Each checkpoint allows you to assess progress and viability of the initiative, and where required, you can move an initiative into a different delivery model with a different (slower or faster) speed.

First Steps for Your Organization

To support you in adopting what I have described in this chapter, I will provide two exercises for you to run in your organization. This time, both of them are highly related: the first is an analysis of your application portfolio and the second is the identification of a minimum viable cluster of application for which a capability uplift will provide real value.

Application Portfolio Analysis

If you are like most of my clients, you will have hundreds or thousands of applications in your IT portfolio. If you spread your change energy across all of those, you will likely see very little progress, and you might ask yourself whether the money is actually spent well for some of those applications. So, while we spoke about the IT delivery process in the chapter 1 exercises as one dimension, the application dimension is the second dimension that is important. Let's look at how to categorize your application in a meaningful way.

Each organization will have different information available about its applications, but in general, an analysis across the following four dimensions can be done:

- Criticality of application: How important is the application for running our business? How impactful would an issue be on the user experience for our customers or employees? How much does this application contribute to regulatory compliance?
- Level of investment in application: How much money will we spend in this application over the next 12–36 months? How much have we spent on this application in

the past? How many priority projects will this application be involved with over the next few years?

- Preferred frequency of change: If the business could choose a frequency of change for this application, how often would that be (hourly, weekly, monthly, annually)? How often have we deployed change to this application in the last 12 months?

- Technology stack: The *technology stack* is important, as some technologies are easier to uplift than others. Additionally, once you have a capability to deliver, for example, Siebel-based applications more quickly, any other Siebel-based application will be much easier to uplift too, as tools, practices, and methods can be reused. Consider all aspects of the application in this technology stack: database, data itself, program code, application servers, and middleware.

For each of the first three dimensions, you can either use absolute values (if you have them) or relative numbers representing a nominal scale to rank applications. For the technology stack, you can group them into priority order based on your technical experience with DevOps practices in those technologies. I recommend using a table with headings much like the one in Table 2.1. On the basis of this information, you can create a ranking of importance by either formally creating a heuristic across the dimensions or by doing a manual sorting. It is not important for this to be precise; we are aiming only for accuracy here.

It's clear that we wouldn't spend much time, energy, and money on applications that are infrequently changed—applications that are not critical for our business and on which we don't intend to spend much money in the future. Unfortunately, just creating a ranking of applications is usually not sufficient, as the IT landscape of organizations is very complex and requires an additional level of analysis to resolve dependencies in the application architecture.

#	Application	Technology	Strategic Application	Frequency of Charge	Size of the Application in the Investment Portfolio
95	App A	Java, .NET, Oracle	4–Critical	9	4–Very High

Table 2.1: Application analysis example: A table like this will help you structure the application analysis

Identifying a Minimum Viable Cluster

As discussed above, the minimum viable cluster is the subset of applications that you should focus on, as an uplift to these will speed up the delivery of the whole cluster. Follow the steps below to identify a minimum viable cluster:

1. Pick one of the highest-priority applications (ideally based on the portfolio analysis from the previous exercise) as your initial application set (consisting of just one application).
2. Understand which other applications need to be changed in order to make a change to the chosen application set.

3. Determine a reasonable cutoff for those applications (e.g., only those covering 80% of the usual or planned changes of the chosen application).
4. You now have a new, larger set of applications and can continue with steps 2 and 3 until the application set stabilizes to a minimum viable cluster.
5. If the cluster has become too large, pick a different starting application or be more aggressive in step 3.

Once you have successfully identified your minimum viable cluster, you are ready to begin the uplift process by implementing DevOps practices such as test automation and the adoption of cloud-based environments, or by moving to an Agile team delivering changes for this cluster.

CHAPTER 3

Dealing with Software Packages and Software Vendors

"If you don't know what you want," the doorman said,
"you end up with a lot you don't."
—**Chuck Palahniuk**, *Fight Club*

In many organizations, the language that describes the software package in use—usually a COTS product that has been chosen for its features—is less than favorable. Clearly this software, often considered legacy, did not magically appear in the organization; someone made the decision to purchase a software package as a response to a business problem. There are good reasons to not reinvent the wheel but leverage packaged software instead. Unfortunately, the state of many software packages these days is such that they don't behave like modern applications should. In this chapter, I will discuss the criteria that you should consider when choosing a software package and how you can work to improve the software package you already have, and I will provide some exercises at the end to adapt these guidelines for yourself. Let's talk first about the idea behind software packages.

The original purpose of software packages was to support commodity processes in your organization. These processes are very similar to those of other organizations and do not differentiate you from your competitors. And even though many of these software packages are now delivered as *software as a service* (SaaS), your organization has legacy package solutions that you have to maintain.

The problem is that many organizations that adopted software packages ended up customizing the product so much that the upgrade path has become expensive. For example, I have seen multiple Siebel upgrades that cost many millions of dollars. When the upgrade path is expensive, it means that newer, better, safer functionality that comes with newer versions of the package is often not available to the organization for years. Besides this downside, heavy customization over time to make the software support all the requirements from business also means that each further change becomes more expensive and that technical debt increases over time.

If we also recognize that the concept of an end-state architecture is not applicable anymore, it becomes clear that software packages should be designed so that they can follow a life cycle that includes eventual decommission for a new, different system by making it easy to decouple them from the rest of the architecture. Every component in the architecture should be seen as temporary so that you are not bound to a specific software vendor. The IT market evolves so quickly that the safe bet today might be a liability in the near future. Dealing with a software package for which the vendor has gone under or where the specific package is not strategic to the vendor anymore is a nightmare, as defect fixes and other support become harder and harder to get. I have been in this situation multiple times and ended up trying to reverse engineer the software in my team to deal with problems, which is expensive and time consuming.

Application architecture is a key factor to determine the speed at which you can deliver and is one of the hardest and slowest things to change. Considering this, the choice of introducing a new software package into your organization should be one that considers the impact to the overall architecture and not something that should be driven purely by functionality alone.

A lot of IT delivery nowadays is closer to assembly with LEGO blocks than it is to handcrafting something with Play-Doh. To allow for this, the applications you leverage should be modular, leveraging an open architecture and good engineering practices so that you can maximize benefits from them. If that's not the case, it would be like having LEGO blocks that all have different connecting mechanisms, so you end up putting glue between the blocks because nothing fits together otherwise. This, of course, defeats the purpose of the module blocks and will make changes to the structure more difficult.

How to Choose the Right Product for Your Organization

Warlike arguments have been fought over which IT product to choose for a project or business function. Should you use SalesForce, Siebel, or Microsoft as your CRM system, for example? Just looking at the functionality is not sufficient anymore, because as much as it should be our preference, it is very unlikely that an organization will use the product as is. The application architecture the product will be part of will continue to evolve, which often requires changes to the software product.

Architecture and engineering principles play a much larger role than in the past due to continuous evolution of the architecture. This puts a very different view on product choice. Of course, the choice is always contextual for each company and each area of business. Your decision framework should guide the decision to make sure all factors are considered. And while the decision might be different for each of you, what I can do is provide a technology decision framework (TDF) that helps you think more broadly about technology choices before you make them.

My TDF is based on three dimensions for you to evaluate: (1) functionality, (2) architecture maturity, and (3) engineering principles.

Functionality

Very often the functionality provided by the software package is the key decision factor. The closer the functionality aligns with the process that you want to support, the better a choice it will be. For you to determine whether a software package is suitable or whether you should build a custom system (which hopefully leverages open-source libraries and modules, so you aren't starting from scratch) requires that you take a good, hard look at your organization. Two factors will be important in this decision: your flexibility in the process you are trying to support and your engineering capabilities. If you are not very flexible and you have a custom-made process, then leveraging a software product will likely require a lot of expensive customizations. If you don't have a strong engineering capability either in-house or through one of your strategic partners, then leveraging a software package is perhaps the better choice. You need to understand where you stand on the continuum from flexible process and low engineering capability (= package) to a custom-made process and high engineering capability (= custom solution).

If you land on the side of a software package, then create an inventory of the required functionality as requirements or *user stories*, and evaluate the candidate packages. Ideally, you want real business users to be involved in the evaluation to make sure it is functionally appropriate for the business. The idea is that a package is giving you a lot right out of the box, and it shouldn't be too much hassle to get a demo installed in your environment for this purpose. If it is a hassle, then that's a warning sign for you.

Architecture Maturity

Application architecture maturity is important to the ongoing support of your application, as a well-architected application will make it easier for you to manage and maintain the application. If you build an application yourself, you will have to deal with architecture considerations, such as scaling and monitoring, and the better your IT capability is, the more you are able to build these architecture aspects yourself. Otherwise, you can choose a package solution to do this for you.

Four aspects that you can use to start the assessment of architecture maturity are as follows:

1. Auto scaling: When your application becomes successful and is being used more, then you need to scale the functions that are under stress. The architecture should intelligently support the flexible scaling of different parts of the application (e.g., not just scale the whole application but rather the functions that require additional scale).

2. Self-healing: When something goes wrong, the application architecture should be able to identify this and run countermeasures. This might mean the traditional restarting of servers/applications, cleaning out message queues, or spinning up a new version of the application/server.

3. Monitoring: You want to understand what is going on with your application. Which elements are being used? Which parts are creating value for your business? To do this, the application architecture should allow you to monitor as many aspects as possible and make that data available externally for your monitoring solution.

4. Capability for change: You want to understand what it takes to make customizations. How modular is the architecture? If there are a lot of common components, this will hinder you from making independent changes and will likely increase your batch size due to dependencies on those common modules. The application architecture should be modular in nature so that you can change

and upgrade components without having to replace the whole system. Backward and forward compatibility are also important to provide flexibility for upgrades.

Engineering Principles

Engineering principles increase in importance the more you believe that the application will have to evolve in the future; and this, in turn, is often driven by the strategic importance of the application for your customer interactions. Good engineering principles in an application allow you to quickly change things and scale up delivery to support increasing volumes of change. The better skilled your IT department is, the more it will be able to leverage these principles and patterns. If you don't have strong IT capabilities, then you will focus more on the built-in architecture features. Here are a few things to look out for:

- Source code management: All code and configuration should be extractable. You want to be able to use enterprise-wide configuration management to manage dependencies between systems. To do that, the exact configuration of an application must be extractable and quickly restorable. Inbuilt or proprietary solutions don't usually allow you to integrate with other applications, hence breaking the ability to have a defined state across your enterprise systems. If necessary, you should be able to re-create the application in its exact state from the external source control system, which is only possible if you can extract the configuration from the application to store it in a *software configuration management (SCM) system*. This means no configuration should be exclusive to the COTS product. The ease with which the extract and import can be done will give you an indication of how well this can be integrated into your delivery life cycle. The extracts should be text based so that SCM systems can compare different versions, analyze differences, and support merge activities as required.

- Automation through APIs: The application should be built with automation in mind and provide hooks (e.g., *application programming interfaces [APIs]*) to fully automate the life cycle. This includes code quality checks, unit testing, compilation, and packaging. None of these activities should have to rely on using a graphical user interface. The same is true for the deployment and configuration of the application in the target environments; there should be no need for a person to log in to the environment for deployment and configuration purposes. As a result of automation, build and deployment times are short (e.g., definitely less than hours, and ideally, less than minutes).

- Modularity of the application: This reduces the build and deployment times, allowing for smaller-scale production deployments and overall smaller batch sizes by reducing the transaction cost of changes. It minimizes the chance of concurrent development and developers having to work on the same code. This, in turn, reduces the risk of complicated merge activities.

- Cloud enablement: First of all, it's not monolithic, so required components can be scaled up and down as needed without engaging the whole application. Licensing is flexible and supports cloud-use cases. Mechanisms are built into the system so that application monitoring is possible at a granular level.

To help you better select the most appropriate product for your needs, score each of the proposed products on the four areas we've discussed: functionality, architecture, engineering capability, and in-house IT capability. I have provided an example scorecard in Table 3.1, which you can use as a starting point for your own evaluation.

		Product A	Product B	Product C
Functionality	Func. Area 1			
	Func. Area 2			
	Func. Area 3			
Architecture	Auto Scaling			
	Self-Healing			
	Monitoring			
	Changeability			
Engineering Capability	Source Code			
	APIs			
	Modularity			
	Cloud Enablement			
In-House IT Capability				

Table 3.1: Example scorecard: New applications should be evaluated on four dimensions, not just functionality

What Do We Do with Our Existing Legacy Applications?

While the advice in the last section is great for introducing new applications, you will still have to deal with your existing legacy application portfolio. I will describe later how to evolve your application architecture if you have control over it. Here, we will look at what you can do if the application is not fully in your control.

You are probably already working with a list of applications, and some of them are supported by software vendors who created the software or made specific changes for you, or both. Yet when you look at the application, it is quite possible that it is not following the modern architecture and engineering principles as I described earlier. You will likely not want to invest in completely replacing these systems immediately, so you have to find other ways to deal with them There are four principle options that I recommend exploring with such software vendors: (1) leverage your system integrators, (2) leverage user groups, (3) strangle the application, and/or (4) incentivize the vendor to improve their product.

Of course, not all vendors and applications are created equally. There are multimillion-dollar organizations that you have to deal with differently than with your small-scale vendor that has only one application to support. I think the four basic patterns apply across the spectrum, but you should tailor them to your context.

Leverage a System Integrator

Having spent my entire career either working for a software vendor or system integrator, I find it surprising that so much is left on the table when it comes to using the relationship effectively beyond the immediate task at hand. If you work with a large *system integrator (SI)* to maintain and develop an application, it is likely that the SI is working with the same application in many other places. While you have some leverage with the software vendor, the SI can use the leverage he has across several clients to influence the application vendor. The better and more aligned your organization is with your SI on how applications should be developed, the easier it will be to successfully influence the software vendor. Better leverage with software application vendors to change their architecture is only one of many benefits that you can derive from changing your relationship with your SI.

Leverage User Groups

For most popular applications, there are user groups, which can be another powerful channel to provide feedback to the vendor. Sometimes these are organized by the vendor itself; sometimes they are independent. In either case, it is worthwhile to find allies who also want to improve the application architecture in line with modern practices. Having a group of clients approach the vendor with the same request can be very powerful. A few years back, I was working with an Agile software that was unable to provide reporting based on *story points*, relying instead on hour tracking. The product vendor always told my client, my colleagues, and me that our request was unique and hence not a high priority for them. We could only get traction once we had reached out to some other organizations that, unsurprisingly, had issued the same request and had received the same response. The vendor was clearly not transparent with us. Once we had found an alliance of customers, the vendor took our feedback more seriously and fixed the problem.

I encourage you to look for these user groups as a way to find potential allies as well as work-arounds and "hacks" that you can leverage in the meantime. By now, people worldwide have solved how to leverage DevOps practices for applications that are not very suitable on paper for the implementation of DevOps. And the good news is that DevOps enthusiasts are usually very happy to share that information.

Fence In Those Applications and Reinvest

As discussed in the previous chapter, when the application is not changing and you have to divest from it, you can use an analogy to the strangler pattern in software development to slowly move away from the application. Reduce the investment in the application and reinvest to build new functionality somewhere else that is more aligned with the architecture you have in mind. Be transparent that you are doing this because the software vendor is not providing the capabilities that you are looking for, but you would reconsider if and when those capabilities were available. This will incentivize the software vendor to look into investing into a better architecture (perhaps the reason that the capabilities don't exist is simply because no one ever asked for them before). Make sure to explain why locked-down architecture and tools are not appropriate going forward and that your requirements for modern architecture require changes in the application architecture. If the software vendor decides that those capabilities are just not the right ones for their application, then not investing any further into the application and spending your money somewhere else is the right thing to do anyway to enable the next evolution of your architecture.

Incentivize the Vendor

I always prefer the carrot over the stick; you, too, should look for win-win situations. Improvements in the architecture and engineering of an application will lead to benefits on your side, which you can use to incentivize the vendor. What is usually even more effective is to show how changes will make the application more attractive for your organization and how more and more licenses will be required over time. This is the ultimate incentive for vendors to improve their architecture. And of course, you can present publicly how great the application is and hence create new customers—a win for both parties.

As I said in the beginning of this chapter, the opinion on software packages in many organizations is not great. It is therefore surprising that organizations do not actively manage what software they do use and how little effort goes into engaging their software vendors to improve the situation. I truly believe that vendors would be happy to come to the party more effectively if more organizations would ask the right questions. After all, why would a software vendor invest in DevOps and Agile–aligned architectures when all every customer is asking for is more functionality and no one is paying for architecture improvements? If companies engaged vendors to discuss the way they want to manage the software package and how important DevOps practices are for them in that process, vendors would invest more to improve those capabilities.

Be Creative

If all else fails and you feel courageous and curious, then you can ignore the guidance from your vendors and attempt to adopt DevOps techniques yourself, even to software products that don't easily lend themselves to those techniques. This is how you start:

- Find and manage the source code, which sounds easier than it often is. You might have to extract the configuration out of a database or from the file system to get to a text-based version of the code.
- Find ways to manage this code with common configuration and code-merge tools rather than the custom-made systems the vendor might recommend. You should also investigate the syntax of the code to see whether there are parts of the code that are non-relevant metadata that you can ignore during the merge process. Something that in Siebel, for example, has saved my team hundreds of hours.
- Try to find APIs or programming hooks in the applications that you can leverage to automate process steps that otherwise would require manual intervention, even if those were meant for other purposes.

In my team, we have used these techniques for applications like Siebel, SAP, Salesforce, and Pega.*

The above techniques will, I hope, help you to better drive your own destiny and be part of a thriving ecosystem where IT is a real enabler. The last piece of the ecosystem that I want to explore is the role of the system integrator, a topic obviously close to my heart, which I'll address in the next chapter.

---

* I wrote a more detailed description of these techniques for the blog *InfoQ*.[1]

First Steps for Your Organization

Determine Guidelines for New Applications

Based on the sample scorecard provided in the Table 3.1, derive a scorecard for your organization. Take the next product decision (or a historic one if nothing is coming up) and apply this scorecard to see how it differs from your current process. Determine whether or not this scorecard, with an architecture focus, provides a different result. I would recommend inviting stakeholders across the organization to a workshop to discuss results and next steps to change your evaluation process going forward.

Strengthen Your Architecture by Creating an Empowering Ecosystem

So, you already have software packages in your organization like so many others. In the previous chapter, we did an analysis of your application portfolio, which you can leverage now to determine which software packages are strategic for your organization.

1. Based on the previous application portfolio analysis (or another means), determine a small subset of strategic applications (such as the first minimum viable cluster) to devise a strategy for creating an empowered ecosystem around them.
2. Now pick these strategic packages and run the scorecard from this chapter. You can largely ignore the functional aspects, as they are used more for the choice between package and custom software. You could, however, use the full scorecard in case you are willing to reconsider whether your current choice is the right one. Given that

you are doing this after the fact, you will already know how suitable the package was by the amount of customizations that your organization has already made.

3. Where you identify weaknesses in your software package, determine your strategy for them. How will you work with the software vendor to improve the capabilities? Will you work with them directly? Will you leverage a system integrator or engage with a user group?

4. Results take time. Determine a realistic review frequency to see whether or not your empowered ecosystem is helping you improve the applications you are working with. You can leverage the principles for measuring technical debt from the previous chapter as a starting point if you don't have any other means to measure the improvements in your packaged applications.

CHAPTER 4

Finding the Right Partner

It's not unlike a marriage, the partnership.
All the effort and good intentions in the world can't make things right
if you choose poorly in the first place.
—**Cecilia Grant**, *A Christmas Gone Perfectly Wrong*

The reality in pretty much every large organization is that you are not working alone. Somewhere in your organization, smaller or larger parts of your IT are either outsourced or at least have an SI helping you deliver the IT that is required to run your business. This must be managed correctly to make sure you retain sufficient IP while getting the benefits from working with an experienced partner.

There is a lot of talk in the industry about how important culture is and that Agile and DevOps are mostly cultural movements. You will hear a lot of stories and examples of how to improve the culture within your organization when you attend conferences or read blogs. I completely agree that your organizational culture is crucial to being successful, but I wonder why there is not more discussion on how to align the cultures of SIs and the organizations they work with. To date, most company–SI relationships are very transactional and driven through vendor management. Words like *partner*, *partnership*, and *collaboration* are often used, yet the results on the ground are too often a misaligned culture due to many reasons.

In this chapter, I want to help improve the situation based on my experience of being on both sides as an SI and as a client of SIs. There are ways to improve the relationship and make it more meaningful. And then there are certain pitfalls that you need to avoid. At the end of the day, both sides want the relationship to be successful—at least that is my experience. It is often a lack of context and limited experience that are preventing us from extending organizational culture beyond the traditional organizational boundaries.

How to Create Beneficial Strategic Partnerships with a System Integrator

Many organizations going down the path of Agile and DevOps determine that the best way to be successful is to transition to Agile and DevOps by initially relying on in-house capabilities due to the higher level of control over your people and the environment they work in (salaries, goals, incentives, policies) than you have over the people of your SI.

Unless you are really willing to take everything back in-house, you will at some stage start working with your SI partners. Fortunately, there are plenty of benefits to working with a partner. The right partner will be able to bring you experience from all the companies they are working with, they have relationships with your product vendors that are deeper than yours, and they can provide an environment that entices talent to join them that you might not be able to provide. IT is at the core of every business nowadays, but not every company can be an IT company. Strategic partnerships allow you to be a bit of both—to have enough intellectual property and insight into the way your system is built and run while permitting your strategic partner to deal with much of the core IT work. Be open and willing to delegate IT when needed in order to maintain balance—and success—overall.

The world of technology is moving very fast, which means we have to learn new technologies all the time. If you have a good relationship with your partner, you might be able to co-invest in new technologies and support the training of your partner's resources; and in return, you might get reciprical benefits in exchange for a credential that the partner can use to showcase their ability with the new technology. My heart warms every time I see a conversation like that take place—where two companies sit together truly as partners to look for win-win situations. Taking an active interest in the world of your partners is important.

In some of my projects I was part of a blended team in which my people's experience in technology worked together with the client's employees' intimate knowledge of the business. Those client teams could maintain and improve the solution long after we left, which is what real success looks like. We not only built a better system but left the organization better off by having upskilled the people in new ways of working. As discussed in the application portfolio chapter, there might be applications where you don't want to build in-house capability and for which this approach does not apply.

For your innovation and workhorse applications, you want to leverage the technology and project experience on the SI side with the business knowledge and continued intellectual property around the IT landscape from your organization. You should avoid having vendors who do not align with your intended ways of working and those whom you don't have visibility into their processes and culture to ensure they align with yours—otherwise, knowledge of your systems sits with individuals from these vendors/contractors, and most changes happen in what appears to be a *black box mode*. This makes it very difficult for you to understand when things go wrong, and when they do, you don't see it coming. One way to avoid this proliferation of vendors and cultures is to have a small number of strategic partners so that you can spend the effort to make the partnerships successful. The fewer the partners, the fewer the variables you most deal with to align cultures. Cultural alignment in ways of working, incentives, values, as well as the required expertise should really be the main criteria for choosing your SI besides costs.

Importance of In-House IP

Your organization needs to understand how IT works and needs to have enough capacity, skill, and intellectual property to determine your own destiny. As we said before, IT is at the core of every business now; a minimum understanding of how this works is important so that you can influence how IT supports your business today, tomorrow, and the day after. But what does it mean to have control of your own destiny in IT? While there are some trends that take "headaches" away from your IT department (think cloud, SaaS, or COTS), there is really no way of completing outsourcing the accountability and risk that comes with IT.

You will also have to think about the tools and processes that your partners bring to the table. It is great that your vendor brings additional tools, methods, and so on, but unless you are able to continue to use those tools and methods after you change vendors, they can become a hindrance later if those tools are critical for your IT delivery. If they are not transparent to you and you don't fully understand how they work, you have to take this into account in your partnering strategy, as you will be bound to them tighter than you might like.

Fortunately, there is a trend toward open methods and standards, which makes it a lot easier to communicate across company barriers. Agile methodologies like the *Scaled Agile Framework (SAFe)* and *Large-Scale Scrum (LeSS)* are good examples. It is likely that you will tailor your own method based on influences from many frameworks. When you make using your method a condition for working with your organization, it helps you keep control. You do, however, need to make sure your methods are appropriate and be open to feedback from your partners. Your partners should absolutely bring their experience to the table and can help you improve your methods.

Standards are also important on the engineering side. Too many organizations have either no influence over or no visibility into how their partners develop solutions. Practices like automatic unit testing, static code analysis, and automated deployments are staples. Yet many organizations don't know whether and to what degree they are being used by their partner. Having the right structure and incentives in place makes it easier for your partner to use those practices, but it is up to you to get visibility into the engineering practices being used for your projects.

One practical way to address this is to have engineering standards for your organizations that every team has to follow no matter what, whether it's in-house, single vendor, or multivendor. These standards will also provide a common language that you can use with your partners to describe your vision for IT delivery (for example, what your definition of continuous integration is). Luckily, there is a lot of work out there that you can leverage to describe these standards; you don't have to reinvent them from scratch. For inspiration, look into popular software engineering books such as *Continuous Delivery: Reliable Software Releases through Build, Test, and Deployment Automation* by Jez Humble and David Farley; *The Pragmatic Programmer: From Journeyman to Master* by Andrew Hunt and David Thomas; and *Release It!: Design and Deploy Production-Ready Software* by Michael T. Nygard.

Changing the "Develop-Operate-Transition" Paradigm

In the past, contracts with system integrators had something mildly Machiavellian to them, where a company creates a terrible work environment in which nobody wins. One of the models that suffers from unintentional consequences over time is the *develop-operate-transition*

(*DOT*) contract. I am not sure how familiar you are with this contract term, so let me quickly explain what I mean. DOT contracts work on the basis that there are three distinct phases to a project: a delivery phase, where the product is created; an operate phase, where the product is maintained by another party; and a transition phase, where the product is brought back in-house.

Many organizations use two different vendors for development and operations, or at least threaten to give the operate phase to someone else while working with a delivery partner. There are a few things wrong with this model. First of all, if you have a partner who is only accountable for delivery, it is only natural that considerations for the operate phase of the project will be less important to them. After all, the operate activities will be done by someone else. The operate party will try to protect their phase of the project on their side, and you will likely see an increasing amount of escalations toward hand-over. There is no ill-intent here, it is just a function of different focuses based on the scope of the contracts.

The second problem is that many DOT projects are run as more or less black box projects, where the client organization is only involved as the stakeholder and, until it gets to the transition phase, has not built internal knowledge on how to run and maintain the system. This causes problems not only during transition but also when navigating misalignments between delivery and operate parties. With just a little tweaking, we can bring this model up to date. Choose a partner that is accountable for both the delivery and operation. You can change the incentive model between the two phases to reflect the different characteristics. Make sure that there is team continuity between phases with your partner, so that people who will operate the solution later are already involved during delivery.

Across the whole project life cycle, embed some of your own people into the team so that you can grow your understanding of the solution and what it took to create and support it. Ideally, have tandem roles where both your partner and your own organization put people in (e.g., project manager, delivery team lead, system architects) to share responsibilities. In this model, the downsides of the old DOT model are addressed, and you can still leverage the overall construct of DOT projects and combine it with DevOps principles. My best projects have used this model, and the results have been long lasting, beyond my involvement.

Cultural Alignment in the Partnership

As mentioned earlier in the book, I have been on both sides of a partnership as a system integrator (SI) providing services to a client and in staff augmentation roles, where I had to work with SIs. It is quite easy to blame the SIs for not doing the right thing—for not leveraging all the DevOps and Agile practices and for not experimenting how to do things better.

The reality is that every person and every organization does what they think is the right thing to do in their context. No one is trying to be bad in software development. Unfortunately, sometimes relationships have been built on distrust: because I don't trust you, I will have a person looking after what you are doing. The vendor then creates a role for someone to deal with that person, and both sides add more process and more documents on each side to cover their backside. More and more process, roles, and so on get introduced until we have several levels of separation between the real work and the people talking to each other from both organizations. To make things worse, all this is just non-value-added activities as payment for the distrust between partners.

But imagine you trusted your SI like you trust the best person on your team. What processes and documents would not be required, and what would that do to the cost and speed of delivery for you? Despite these potential advantages, there is way too little discussion on how to make the relationship work. How could we create a joint culture that incentivizes all partners to move toward a more Agile and DevOps way of working, and how do we do this when we have long-lasting relationships with contracts already in place?

First of all, I think it is important to understand your partner; as in any good marriage, you want to know what works and what doesn't work for your partner. And when I say *partner*, I mean partner. If you do the off project with a vendor and it is purely transactional, then you don't have to worry about this. But if you work with the same company for many years and for some of your core systems, then it does not make sense to handle them transactionally. You want to build a partnership and have a joint DevOps-aligned culture.

In a real partnership, you understand how the SI defines his or her success, and both sides are open about what they want from the relationship. Career progression has been one of those examples, and I have been lucky, as most of my clients understood when I discussed the career progression of my people with them and why I needed to move people out of their current roles. From a company perspective, they would have preferred to keep my guy in the same role for many years; but for me, that would not have been good, as my people would have looked for opportunities somewhere else.

Of course, all of this goes both ways, so you should not accept if the SI wants to behave like a black box—you want the relationship to be as transparent as you feel is right. You have the choice to buy a "service" that can be a black box with only the interface defined. In this case, you don't care how many people work on it or what they are doing; you just pay for the service. This gives the SI the freedom to run independently—a model that works well for SaaS—and you might have some aspects of your IT that can work with a XaaS mind-set.

For other projects that include working with your core IT systems and with people from your organization or other third parties, you want transparency. A vendor that brings in their own tools and methods is basically setting you up for a higher transition cost when you want to change. You should have your own methods and tools, and each SI can help you improve this from their experience. You don't want any black box behavior. Fortunately, common industry frameworks such as SAFe or Scrum do help get to a common approach across organizations with little ramp-up time.

Thinking about partnerships, you should remember that you cannot outsource risk. I have often seen that the client is just saying "well, that's your problem" when an SI brings up a possible situation. The reality is that if the project fails, the client will be impacted. Just closing your eyes and ears and making it the SI's problem will not make it go away. Think of the disaster with the Australian census, where the delivery partner took a lot of negative publicity,[1] or Healthcare.gov in the United States, where vendors blamed each other for the problems.[2] Even if the vendors were at fault, the organizations took a huge hit in reputation in both cases; and given that they were public services, it created a lot of negative press.

Partnership Contracts

In Agile, we want flexibility and transparency. But have you structured your contracts in a way that allows for this? You can't just use the same fixed-price, fixed-outcome contract where every change has to go through a rigorous change control process. Contracts are often structured with certain assumptions, and moving away from them means trouble. Time and materials for Agile contracts can cause problems because they don't encourage adherence to outcomes—something that is only okay if you have a partner experienced with Agile and a level of maturity and trust in your relationship.

Agile contracts require you to take more accountability and be more actively involved in the scope management. In my experience, the best Agile contracts are the ones that are built on the idea of fixed capacity aligned to some outcome and flexible scope (the delivery of a number of features for which some details are defined as the project progresses).

There are ways to create Agile contracts that work for all parties, so let's explore some basics of a typical Agile project. While Agile encourages teams to deliver production-ready code with each sprint, the reality often means that the delivery process is broken down into four phases:

1. scope exploration up front and ongoing refinement (*definition of ready*)
2. sprint/iteration delivery of user stories (*definition of done*)
3. release readiness preparation/*hardening* and transition to production (definition of done-done)
4. post-go-live support/warranty (definition of done-done-done)

With that in mind, a contract should reflect these four phases. As a departure from the common deliverable- or phase-based pricing, where your partner is being paid based on deliverable (such as design documents) or completion of a project phase (such as design or development), these contracts reflect user stories as units of work. Each story goes through the four phases described above, and payments should be associated with that; a certain percentage should be paid as a story achieves the definition of ready and the different levels of done. Here is a sample breakdown that works well:

- We have three hundred story points to be delivered in three iterations and one release to production: $1,000 total price.
- A payment schedule of 10%/40%/30%/20% (first payment at kickoff, second one as stories are done in iterations, third one once stories are released to production, last payment after a short period of warranty).
- Signing contract: 10% = $100.

- Iteration 1 (50 pts. done): $50/300 \times 0.4 \times 1{,}000 = \$66$.
- Iiteration 2 (100 pts. done): $100/300 \times 0.4 \times 1{,}000 = \$133$.
- Iteration 3 (150 pts. done): $150/300 \times 0.4 \times 1{,}000 = \$201$.
- Hardening and go-live: 30% = $300.
- Warranty complete: 20% = $200.

With this contract model in place, we have a contractual model that ties the delivery of scope to the payments to the vendor. In my experience, this model is a good intermediate point of having flexibility while only paying for working scope. There are things that you want to provide as part of the contract too: an empowered product owner who can make timely decisions, a definition of the necessary governance, and a work environment that supports Agile delivery (physical workspace, IT, infrastructure, etc.). Very mature organizations can utilize time and material contracts as they operate with their own mature methodology to govern the quality and quantity of outcome; less mature organizations benefit from the phased contract outlined above.

Another aspect of contracts is aligned incentives. Let's start with a thought experiment: You have a really good working relationship with an SI over many years, but somehow, with all the legacy applications you are supporting together, you didn't invest in adopting DevOps practices. You now want to change this. You agree on a co-investment scheme and quickly agree on a roadmap for your applications. A few months in, you see the first positive results with demos of continuous integration and test automation at your regular showcases. Your SI approaches you at your regular governance meeting and says he wants to discuss the contract with you, as the average daily rate of his overall team has changed. What do you expect to see? That the average daily rate of a worker has gone down thanks to all the automation? I mean, it should be cheaper now, shouldn't it?

Well, let's look at it together. The average daily rate is the average rate calculated on the basis that less-skilled work is cheaper and work that requires more skills or experience is paid higher. The proportion of those two to each other determines the average daily rate. When we automate, what do we automate first? Of course: the easier tasks that require fewer skills. The automation itself usually requires a higher level of skill. Both of these mean that the proportion of higher-skilled work goes up and, with it, the average daily rate. Wait . . . does that mean things become more expensive? No. Since we replaced some work with automation, in the long run, it will be cheaper overall. If you evaluate your SIs based on the average daily rate, you have to change your thought process. It is overall cost, not daily rates, that matters.

The diagram in Figure 4.1 might help you visualize this counterintuitive outcome. While the average daily rate increased for the same piece of work (relative proportion of higher-cost work increases), the total cost decreased (as there is less overall work to be performed manually). Too many organizations use average daily rate to evaluate their partners and hence incentivize a push for more low-skilled manual labor instead of increased automation. Automation is actually a win-win scenario, as the systems integrator reduces their risk from manual activites while maintaining higher average day rates. At the same time, the client also benefits from the reduced risk and a lower overall cost point.

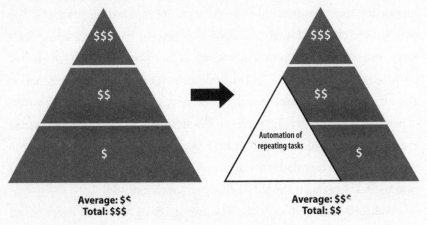

Figure 4.1: Overall costs versus daily rates: Automating work reduces overall cost but increases average cost rate

Partnerships from the SI Side

I also want to look at the company–service provider relationship from the other side—the side of the system integrator. This perspective is not spoken about much, but given that it is usually *my* side, I want to show you how we think and what our challenges are.

The influence of DevOps culture has started to transform relationships to be more open. Even in the request for proposal processes, I can see an increased openness to discuss the scope and approach to delivery. I have worked with government clients for whom, during the process, I was able to help them shift the request to something more aligned with what they were after by adopting an Agile contract like the one I mentioned earlier. Originally, they wanted to pay per deliverable, something unsuitable for Agile delivery. Together, we can usually come up with something that works for all parties and makes sure you get what you are after.

As system integrators, we are still relegated too often to talking to procurement departments that are not familiar with modern software delivery. Contracts are set up with such efficiency that there is no room for experimentation, and where some experimentation is accepted, only positive results are "allowed." If you think about your relationship with SIs, I am sure you can think of ways to improve the relationship and culture to become more open and aligned with your goals. I have added a little test to diagnose your culture alignment in the exercises of this chapter.

Partner Evaluation

I want to spend the last part of this chapter on partner evaluation. Clearly, you don't want your partner to just take your money and provide a suboptimal service to your organization. So what can you do to govern the relationship while considering the open culture you are trying to achieve?

And how do you do that while still having means to intervene if the performance deteriorates?

In the example of a project being done by one SI, you can use a balanced scorecard that considers a few different aspects:

One of them is delivery; in this area, you care about quality and predictability of delivery. How many defects slip into production, how accurate is the delivery forecast, and how are the financials tracking? You might also want to add the evaluation of delivery quality by stakeholders, potentially as an internal net promoter score (*NPS*, which quantifies the percentage of people recommending your service) of business stakeholders. Cycle time and batch size are two other metrics you should care about to improve the overall flow of work through your IT.

The second aspect is technical excellence. At a bare minimum, you want to look at the compliance with your engineering methods (unit testing, test automation, continuous integration, continuous delivery . . .). If your delivery partner is taking shortcuts, technical debt will keep increasing, and at some stage, you will have to pay it down. In my experience, clients do a good job checking the quality of the end product but often fail to govern the engineering pratices that prevent technical debt from accruing. Providing a clear set of expectations around engineering methods and regular inspection (e.g., showcases for test and deployment automation, code reviews, etc.) reduces the chances of further technical debt. I have had great discussions about engineering strategies with clients during such showcases.

The third aspect is throughput; you can approach this from a story point or even stories per release perspective. I assume, though, that your releases will change in structure as your capabilities mature. In light of this, cycle time and batch size are better measures. The interesting aspect of cycle time is that if you optimize for speed, you tend to get quality and cost improvements for free, as discussed earlier.

You should also reserve a section of the scorecard for improvements. Which bottlenecks are you currently improving, and how are you measuring against your predictions? You can add costs per service here (e.g., the cost of a deployment or a go-live) to see specific improvements for salient services in your organization.

Last but not least, you should have a section for the interests of your partner. Career progression, predictability, and market recognition come to mind as some of the noncommercial aspects of the relationship. Of course, revenue and profitability are two other areas of interest that you want to talk about from a qualitative perspective—is this a relationship that is beneficial for both? I recommend having a section of the scorecard where you track two or three priorities from the partner perspective and evaluate those together on a regular basis.

First Steps for Your Organization

Horses for Courses—Determining the Partners You Need

This whole chapter is about finding the right partner that fits your ambition and culture. But the truth is that you probably need different partners for different parts of your portfolio. If you have done the application portfolio activity in chapter 2, this exercise will be easier. There are three different types of applications for the purpose of this exercise:

- Differentiator applications: These applications are evolving very quickly, are usually directly exposed to your customers, and define how your company is perceived in the marketplace.
- Workhorses: These applications drive the main processes in your organizations, such as customer relationship management, billing, finance, and supply-chain processes. They are often referred to as enterprise or legacy systems.

They might not be directly exposed to the customer, but the company derives significant value from these applications and continues to make changes to them to support the evolving business needs.

- True legacy: These applications are pretty stable and don't require a lot of changes. In general, they tend to support your more stable, main processes or some fringe aspects of your business.

Based on these classifications, review your partner strategy to see whether you need to change either the partner itself or the way you engage with the existing one. For the first two categories, you want to engage strategic partners. For legacy applications, you are looking for a cost-effective partner who gets paid for keeping the system running. The incentives for your strategic partners are different. Your partners for the workhorse applications should be evaluated by the efficiencies they can drive into those applications; for the differentiator applications, you want someone who is flexible and will co-invent with you. The outcome of this activity will feed into the second exercise for this chapter.

Run a Strategic Partners Workshop
for Your Workhorse Applications

Organizations spend the majority of their money on their workhorse applications. This makes sense, as these applications are the backbone of the business. For this exercise, I want you to invite your strategic partners who support your workhorse applications (and possibly the differentiator ones) to a workshop. You can do this with all of the partners together, which can be more difficult, or by running separate workshops for each partner. It is important to tell them to assume that the current contract structure is negotiable and to be open-minded for the duration of the workshop.

The structure of this workshop should be as follows:

- Explain to your partner what is important for you in regard to priorities in your business and IT.
- Discuss how you can measure success for your priorities.
- Let your partner explain what is important for them in their relationship with you and what they require in their organization to see the relationship as successful.
- Workshop how you can align your interests.
- Brainstorm what the blocks are to truly achieve a win-win arrangement between your two organizations.

The key to this workshop is that both sides are open-minded and willing to truly collaborate. In my experience, it will take a few rounds of this before barriers truly break down—don't be discouraged if all of the problems are not solved in one workshop. Like everything else we talk about, it will be an iterative process, and it is possible that you will realize that you don't have the right partners yet and need to make some changes in the makeup of your ecosystem.

Do a Quick Self-Check about Your Partnering Culture
A quick test to evaluate your DevOps culture with your system integrator:

- Are you using average daily rate as indicator of productivity, value for money, and so on?
  +1 if you said no.

- Do have a mechanism in place that allows your SI to share benefits with you when he improves through automation or other practices?

  +1 if you said yes. You can't really expect the SI to invest in new practices if there is no upside for him. And yes, there is the "morally right thing to do" argument, but let's be fair. We *all* have economic targets, and not discussing this with your SI to find a mutually agreeable answer is just making it a bit a too easy for yourself, I think.

- Do you give your SI the "wiggle room" to improve and experiment, and do you manage the process together?

  +1 if you said yes. You want to know how much time the SI spends on improving things by experimenting with new tools or practices. If she has just enough budget from you to do exactly what you ask her to do, then start asking for an innovation budget and manage it with her.

- Do you celebrate or at least acknowledge the failure of experiments?

  +1 if you said yes. If you have an innovation budget, are you okay when the SI comes back to let you know that one of the improvements didn't work? Or are you just accepting successful experiments? I think you see which answer aligns with a DevOps culture.

- Do you know what success looks like for your SI?

  +1 if you said yes. Understanding the goals of your SI is important, not just financially but also for the people who work for the SI. Career progression and other aspects of HR should be aligned to make the relationship successful.

- Do you deal with your SI directly?

+1 if you said yes. If there is another party involved, such as your procurement team or an external vendor, then it's likely that messages get misunderstood. And there is no guarantee the procurement teams know the best practices for DevOps vendor management. Are you discussing any potential hindrance in the contracting space directly with your SI counterpart?

If you score 0–2 points, you have a very transactional relationship with your SI and should consider getting to know him or her better to improve the relationship. If you score 3–4 points, you are doing okay but with room for improvements, so you could run a partner workshop to address the other dimensions. If you score 5 or 6 points, you are up ahead with a real partnership that will support you through your transformation. Well done!

Part A Conclusion

This concludes part A, which is about creating a thriving ecosystem for good IT delivery. The material in this first part is of strategic nature, which means changes here will take time and require efforts across your whole organization. Don't try to change everything today—I'd rather you understand the ideas in this part of the book, do some of the activities, and then, as you put your plans together for the next year, next quarter, or next month, start addressing some of the things you've learned. None of these are quick fixes, so steady wins the race. In the next part, I will talk about the people dimension. People are at the center of everything you do, so providing them with the right support is crucial to your success.

PART B
The People and Organizational Dimension

In part B of this book, I want us to look at what is at the core of everything we do: our people. Without people, nothing would happen in our organizations. The challenge, of course, is that most of your people have been exposed to the legacy way of working. You have legacy applications that people tend to complain about, but you likely also have "legacy people with a legacy mind-set." So, how do you shift your workforce away from this legacy way of thinking? And how do you structure your organization in the most supportive way for good delivery outcomes? Part B of this book will look at a few different aspects of legacy thinking that you need to break or shift.

Barry Schwartz made a great point in his March 2014 TED talk when he said that the systems we create will create the workers that operate best in this system.[1] If we create a structure that requires "dumb," repetitive work, we will create "dumb" workers who can only do repetitive work like the assembly line worker of the past. I think we need to create IT organizations that embed the kind of thinking that Dan Pink talks about in his presentation analysis of what motivates people: autonomy, mastery, and purpose.[2] They want the autonomy to make their own choices, they want mastery of skills so that they feel like they know what they are doing, and they want purpose to understand why they are doing what they are doing. Over time, all the people who work in our organizations will then do more meaningful and rewarding work—the coveted win-win scenario. You will see the thread of addressing those three aspects all through part B of the book.

In part B, I will discuss how to provide your people with the right context for their decisions, what team structure you should choose to enable autonomy and purpose, how to shift from legacy thinking that has caused many test automation projects to fail, and how to manage your people better in the post-factory world.

Someone once told me that life would be so easy if we didn't have to deal with other people. Given that this is not an option unless you can afford your own island, let's look at how we can make it easier to deal with people by giving them the right context.

CHAPTER 5

Context is King

Wisdom is intelligence in context.

—**Raheel Farooq**

O ne of the goals of Lean practices is to eliminate waste. But as we've already discussed, the components and outputs of manufacturing are more visible than those of IT, meaning that in manufacturing, the identification of waste is somewhat easier than in the IT world. In manufacturing, we can physically see scrap material, we can see the products that are in storage, we can count the items currently in progress, and when a machine is idle, we can easily see that. In IT, we are dealing with non-physical items, which makes some of this more difficult to do. And if an IT worker is idle, we don't usually notice it, as she will find something to do. Or to say it with Parkinsons' law, "Work expands so as to fill the time available for its completion."

The best way to enable all our workers to eliminate wasteful activities or idle time in IT is for them to understand the context of their work. This will allow them to make their own decisions instead of waiting idly until a decision is being made somewhere else in the organization. It will also enable them to make the right decisions to avoid spending effort on activities that don't lead to the right outcomes. This aligns very well with Dan Pink's motivational factors, as context will allow your people to make autonomous decisions and understand the purpose of the work they are doing.

In our legacy-inspired organization, we believed in the manufacturing approach to delivery, where handovers between machines are not hindering the outcome as long as they are part of a well-defined process. A machine or assembly worker does not need to know why he screws a screw into the metal plate at exactly this position. There is no alternative solution to having the screw in the exact right spot, so that context is not as important.

In IT, context does matter, as coding a specific functionality only works if you understand the context in which the function will be used. I was a developer myself, and when you are limited by the technical design without context, you aren't able to solve problems that arise. But if you understand the context, you can develop a solution to solve the problem even when the design is flawed.

When companies embark on projects, they spend time elaborating on the idea for the project, build a business case for it, and in many cases, spend a lot of time maturing it before it can be kicked off. A lot of context is being created, yet in many organizations, this context is then transferred to the project team purely as documentation. And to make things worse, the project team usually spins up over time so that testers who join later will only learn the context from outdated documentation and "games of telephone."

Furthermore, it is important to note that with any handover, some context will always be lost. Unfortunately, no amount of comments and documentation will ever really provide the full context, which I experienced when getting code back that still did not solve the problem I encountered as functional tester and had documented in a defect record.

Yet passing on context information—even if some of it will be lost in the process—is crucial. People make decisions based on their context and incentive. It is rare that someone involved in a project makes a bad decision due to malevolence; it's usually because he did what he thought to be right with the context he had. So, how can we create a shared context to make the right decisions?

I learned from many successful Agile projects/programs/initiatives that a discovery phase can solve this problem. Having such a discovery activity for a project or feature, or whatever the right unit of work is, provides an investment that pays back over time. I will use the example of a finite Agile project that runs over multiple releases, but you can adopt the same for any project size.

A discovery workshop that can take anywhere from a few hours to many weeks is best broken down into three separate phases:

- understanding the business problem
- finding a viable solution to the problem
- planning delivery and getting ready

Understanding the Business Problem

The first part of discovery is to get the team and stakeholders on the same page. To do this, you have to gather together as many of the people who will deliver the solution involved as is feasible. For a small delivery team, this should actually be the whole team. I have run Agile initiatives that required several dozen people in the delivery teams; in that case, I would invite representation from all the different teams and skills involved (e.g., developers, business analysts, testers, people from the mainframe team, people from the Java team). You can easily run the session with around thirty people in the room. (SAFe provides mechanisms for even larger teams with the *PI* [program increment] *planning* ceremony.) The focus of the first part of discovery is to understand what the team is coming together to solve.

Given that almost all initiatives in an organization require a business case to get funding, the business case is usually a good starting point. The sponsor presents the business case to the team so that everyone knows what has been promised and how success will be measured. While each discovery is tailored to the specific context, here are a few of the many common activities that help to set this context and solidify understanding of the business problem:

- Current and aspired customer/stakeholder experience: This is very helpful to explain what impact the initiative will have to the people who matter most: your customers. This can take the form of process designs, impact maps, customer journeys, or value stream maps. (If you are not familiar with these techniques, a quick Google search will provide plenty of advice.)
- Personas: Some teams make the customer come to life even more by creating personas that can be used all through the delivery phase to write the user stories. Some of my teams went all out with personas—to the point that you nearly believed the persona was part of the team.
- Elevator pitch: You should create an elevator pitch or mission statement that focuses the team on what you are trying to achieve. This might evolve over time but will be an anchor that you keep coming back to.
- In-scope/out-of-scope lists: Some elements are as important in Agile as they were in traditional delivery, so don't forget to have an activity to identify what is in scope and, more importantly, out of scope.
- Risks and issues: Have a discussion to identify risks, issues, and their mitigation.
- Dependencies: Do an initial brainstorm of dependencies internal to your organization and external to it.

- Stakeholder management approach: Stakeholders are crucial for the success of any project. You can deliver the perfect solution, but if your stakeholders are unhappy, you have ultimately failed. To address this, I like to run a stakeholder management workshop to identify who will be impacted by the project and how the team will communicate with them. In Agile, we have richer communication channels than in traditional projects; and in this workshop, you want to leverage this: Who will be invited to showcases and planning sessions? Who will be part of backlog grooming sessions? And to whom do we send recordings of the demos? Be selective in your choices, as meetings can become pretty chaotic if too many stakeholders are part of them. Showcases, especially, can be distracted by too many stakeholders having "good ideas" for additional or changed scope.
- Prioritization and success criteria: My personal favorite in the discovery sessions I run is the discussion around prioritization and success criteria. In Agile, all scope is prioritized in a stack ranking to avoid the problem of having 90% of all scope being "must-haves." Clearly identifying the criteria that will be used for prioritization can be a difficult discussion with business and IT stakeholders, but it will become something that you keep returning to during delivery to keep people on the same page and to make decisions more objective. Too often, projects get derailed by "pet requirements" from senior stakeholders that are based on subjective preference instead of objective outcomes. The same is true for success criteria: what will the organization use after go-live to evaluate whether the project was successful? Try to resist the temptation to use the "I know it when I see it" approach. You want to find at least a couple of quantifiable measures of success; and of course, part of your project should be to operationalize the measurement itself and to define a baseline. It is an unfortunate reality in IT today

that too few projects are actually evaluated post-go-live for their success. This becomes easier when teams become product/service teams and do not exist just for projects anymore but have ongoing ownership of the product/service.

Finding a Viable Solution to the Problem

Now that the team understands the context of the project, we can dive into finding a solution for the problem. Of course, you will have done some of this already when you created the business case (after all, you needed to identify who to involve in the discovery session). It is likely you have a good idea which applications will be impacted and you have a high-level solution in mind on which the business case was based.

This part of discovery can feel a bit chaotic, as it has a strong exploratory dimension to it. You want everyone to collaborate in finding the most appropriate solution to your problem. To do this, you want to do a bit of *to-be process design* and identify the technical architecture of the solution. Where required, you can do deep dives into parts of the process or into specific technologies. This is a great way to identify risks and validate assumptions about what a technology can do for you. Where residual concerns exist, you might already identify spikes that you want to run during delivery.

You will have to find the right balance for your organization between documenting this in detail and having no documentation at all; too much documentation wastes time and effort, while no documentation at all will make it difficult to guide the solution during the project. I recommend diagrams on whiteboards, on PowerPoint slides, or in Visio as a good starting point. High-level architecture should be something that fits on a whiteboard and is documented—and not just in people's heads.

The process-design and technical-architecture workshops will have an *iterative character* as you keep revisiting them to make improvements as the solution evolves during discovery. You created a rich context in the first part of discovery, so keep referring to it to make sure you are focusing on the right things, respecting the scope constraint and everything else defined before. In some cases, you might decide to change outputs from the first part, which is okay too. Once you have done this a few times, you will be amazed by how often the outputs of the first part allow you to steer the discussion to a fruitful outcome. A little hint here: paste the outcomes of the first part on the wall so that they are always visible.

You will also want to start writing up the features of the solution which you might structure under related epics. This list can already be exhaustive or you can leave yourself some room for additional features to be identified. What you need to define in all cases is the *minimum viable product* (*MVP*). What is the minimum amount of scope that needs to be completed before you can go live? This will feature prominently later, when the release planning happens. The tendency is to make the MVP too large, so challenge yourself to keep culling scope until it is truly minimal. In large organizations with complex architecture, my guiding rule is that an MVP needs to be deliverable within three months. Your mileage might vary, though.

But wait, you say, shouldn't Agile be flexible? Why are we defining the solution in discovery and not just letting it emerge through the iterations? In my experience from working in large organizations, I can tell you that you need some guardrails. I have seen projects get derailed for months when, after three iterations, stakeholders decided to move functionality from the CRM system to the ERP system. The team structures had to change and commercial constructs were impacted, as were test strategies and many more things. This extreme idea of flexibility is beyond what an initiative can absorb. Think about discovery as an outline of the *Mona Lisa*, that you will fill in with details during delivery. You want to avoid ending up with a picture of an abstract depiction of love when you were after a picture of a gorgeous lady.

Discovery ————————————————————————→ **Delivery**

Figure 5.1: Discovery versus delivery: Discovery is like the first outline of a picture; delivery fills in the details

Planning Delivery and Getting Ready

After setting the context and finding a viable solution, the last part of discovery is about getting ready for delivery. This part is crucial and will probably take you a while to do, as it involves mobilizing teams, setting up your workspace, estimating the work ahead, and planning the release schedule. This part tends to require less involvement from the business stakeholders and is heavier on the IT delivery team.

Depending on where your organization is with regard to the adoption of Agile and DevOps, the first thing to align is the terminology, methodology, and practices you will use on the project. I personally prefer to use an industry-wide framework such as the Scaled Agile Framework (SAFe), as it provides common terminology and practices as an easy starting point. Of course, you can leverage your own methodology or define a new one. A couple of words of warning, though: If you choose to rename a term because you don't like the sound of it (e.g., from Scrum master to delivery facilitator, which I had to do for a client), then you lose the ability to get guidance from the community. After all, you cannot Google that term, and other people outside your company will not understand you either. The other thing that I am very passionate about is a common structure for your scope hierarchy. I can show you the scars of what happens when you don't have that. If you use

- story > feature > epic
- product backlog item (PBI) > epic > theme
- story > theme > epic

in the same organization, it will, at some stage, lead to confusion. This is flexibility for the sake of flexibility at the cost of organizational effectiveness. Eventually, these terms will collide, so just choose one and stick to it. After all, it's just terminology; consistency is much more important than personal preference. You might also want to run training sessions for the team, the product owner, and any other key roles during this time.

There are other crucial things to define before you start:

- your initial team structure
- your technical practices (continuous integration or continuous delivery, for example)
- your ideal release structure (monthly, weekly, daily. . .)
- how your technical ecosystem will look

Especially in an organization with a lot of legacy applications, the technical ecosystem becomes important. Environments are usually limited and you have to orchestrate delivery with other parts of the organization, so understanding what is available to you becomes a critical element for success.

This is also the right time to do the initial estimation of the project scope, for which you can use planning poker or other Agile estimation practices to start preparing the backlog. You will need to "prime the pump" so that there is enough defined scope for the first few iterations that complies with the "definition of ready" for the team to be successful and effective. There will be ongoing backlog grooming, but in my experience, it takes a while before the grooming can keep up with delivery. I've had many teams run out of scope during delivery; then the team becomes distracted and inefficient as they take in unready scope, search for scope down the backlog, or—worse still—spin their wheels for a while. Having two to three iterations' worth of scope ready to go usually provides enough runway for the team to get the backlog grooming to the right speed.

Discovery ends with two large activities that require preparation, the *discovery showcase* and the planning event (or PI planning if you follow SAFe). The showcase shares the outcomes of discovery with the rest of the organization. It is usually a one- to two-hour session highlighting the outputs from discovery. The planning event brings together the delivery team and stakeholders to plan the first few months. The focus here is on dependencies between teams, having a baseline of goals per iteration, and release and joint-risk management. (The guidelines for PI planning on the SAFe site are quite good.) You want to make sure that your organization is ready across both business and IT. You want to make sure that the content for the PI planning has been prepared and that you have the right facilities to conduct the session, especially when technology is required to communicate across multiple locations.[1] Some people might also be familiar with the term "big room planning" from Lean, which achieves the same by having all teams plan together in a large room, forcing collaboration across teams and frequent communication across organizational boundaries.[2]

Once you have gone through discovery, the team that will deliver the solution has a rich context to work within. It will allow the team and each individual to make decisions that are more likely to be correct. Thinking back to the Dan Pink means for motivation, we have provided autonomy by allowing the team to be part of the decision-making process during discovery (especially during planning and estimation, with which they are less involved in traditional approaches); we gave them purpose by interacting with the business stakeholders and spending time understanding the business problem and impact on customers. Context is also important in regard to the last aspect: mastery.

Mastery requires context and understanding of the area that we are trying to master. One challenge to achieve mastery is a cognitive bias called the Dunning–Kruger effect, which is sometimes also called "illusionary superiority effect."[3] The Dunning–Kruger effect occurs when you don't know what good looks like (e.g., have the right context for your assessment) but you think you are pretty good at it, which explains why we so very often declare victory early. Look at all the organizations that seem to evaluate agility by how many Post-it notes are visible in their offices. I often encounter this when doing maturity assessments, where the teams with the lowest maturity claim to do practices that they don't fully understand, and where the high-maturity teams see a lot of possible improvements and rate themselves low in maturity.

I have learned about Dunning–Kruger the hard way. As a consultant, I am frequently asked to do maturity assessments. Given you usually have to rely on asking questions, you can easily be encountering Dunning–Kruger. Here is how that would go:

Me: Are you using continuous integration?
Developer: Yes, we do.
Me: [Thinking, Okay, I could check the yes box, but let's be sure.] How do you know you are using continuous integration?
Developer: We have a Jenkins server.
Me: And what do you do with Jenkins?
Developer: We build our application.
Me: How often does the Jenkins server build your application?
Developer: Well . . . it runs about once a week, on the weekend.
Me: [Phew!] Okay, there is some more education to be done before this assessment makes sense.

Together with one of my clients, we realized that a self-assessment would not provide us with the right results due to the Dunning–Kruger effect and came up with an alternative approach. Taking a lesson from my university days, when I spent too much time playing a computer game called *Civilization*, we used the idea of a technology tree, which provides guidance for the different technologies required in order to research the next one (e.g., you need astronomy before navigation becomes reliable).[4]

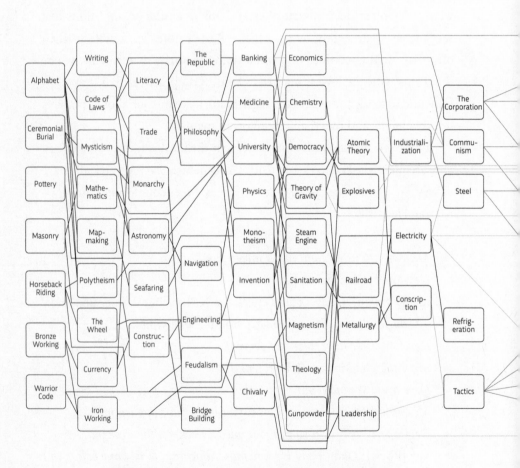

Figure 5.2a: Technology tree: Example showing dependencies between technologies

In our continuous delivery technology tree, we provided context to the teams that described the dependencies between practices (for example, that continuous integration required automated builds—builds triggered from check-in and automated unit tests). This, in turn, allowed teams to assess themselves in the context of the full technology tree, making it easier for them to chart their way to mastery across the tree.

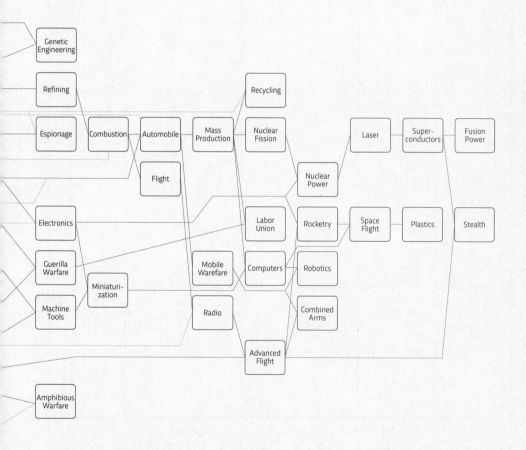

Figure 5.2a, cont.

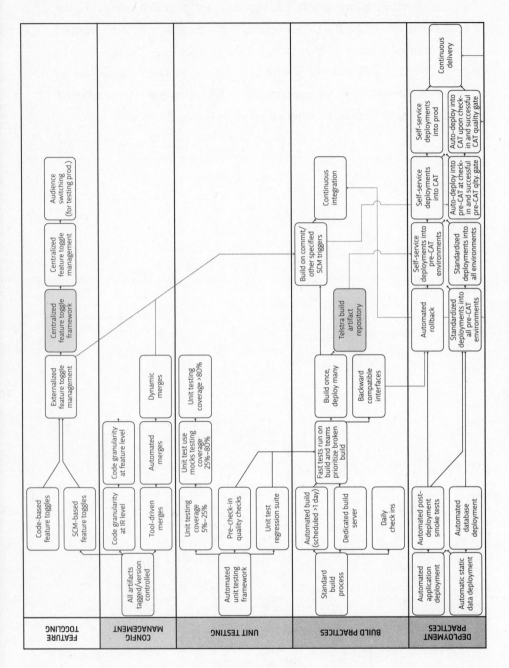

Figure 5.2b: DevOps technology tree showing dependencies

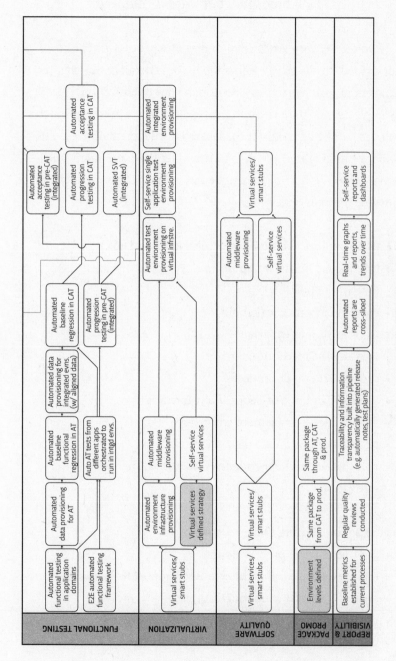

FUNCTIONAL TESTING

- Automated functional testing in application domains
- E2E automated functional testing framework
- Automated data provisioning for AT
- Automated baseline functional regression in AT
- Auto AT tests from different apps orchestrated to run in intgd envs.
- Automated data provisioning for integrated evns. (w/ aligned data)
- Automated baseline regression in CAT
- Automated progression testing in pre-CAT (integrated)
- Automated acceptance testing in pre-CAT (integrated)
- Automated progression testing in CAT
- Automated SVT (integrated)
- Automated acceptance testing in CAT

VIRTUALIZATION

- Virtual services/ smart stubs
- Automated environment infrastructure provisioning
- Virtual services defined strategy
- Automated middleware provisioning
- Self-service virtual services
- Automated test environment provisioning on virtual infrstre.
- Self-service single application test environment provisioning
- Automated integrated environment provisioning

SOFTWARE QUALITY

- Virtual services/ smart stubs
- Virtual services/ smart stubs
- Automated middleware provisioning
- Self-service virtual services
- Virtual services/ smart stubs

PACKAGE PROMO

- Environment levels defined
- Same package from CAT to prod.
- Same package through AT, CAT & prod.

REPORT & VISIBILITY

- Baseline metrics established for current processes
- Regular quality reviews conducted
- Traceability and information transparency built into pipeline (e.g. automatically generated release notes, test plans)
- Automated reports are cross-siloed
- Real-time graphs and reports, trends over time
- Self-service reports and dashboards

Figure 5.2b, cont.

First Steps for Your Organization

Run a Discovery Workshop for an Initiative of Your Choice
I described the discovery workshop in some detail in this chapter, and I encourage you to run a session in your organization. Here is a sample agenda for a two-week long discovery workshop, which you can adjust as required for larger or smaller initiatives. The activities highlighted are just an example; there are many additional activities that you can embed in your discovery sessions to enhance the experience.

Part 1: Explore the Business Problem (Two Days)
- briefing by initiative sponsor (leveraging the business case where possible)
- current customer/stakeholder experience
- to-be customer experience workshop
- creating the mission statement
- success criteria definition
- in-scope and out-of-scope brainstorming
- stakeholder management workshop
- prioritization-scheme discussion
- risks, issues, and dependencies identification and mitigation

Part 2: Solutioning (Three Days)
- high-level to-be process design
- high-level technical architecture to support to-be design
- breaking the scope up into features
- identification of minimum viable product (MVP)
- selected deep dives into technologies and processes

Part 3: Planning for Delivery (Five Days)

- Agile training (if required)
- team structure definition
- estimation of scope
- high-level roadmapping
- technical preparation (environment, quality, configuration management strategies)
- setting up delivery governance
- social contract
- prepping the backlog
- discovery showcase to the organization
- planning workshop (PI planning when using SAFe)

CHAPTER 6

Structuring Yourself for Success

No one has ever restructured themselves out of a problem.
—**Anonymous**

Despite the opening quote, which I love and which so many organizations seem to ignore, I think a bad organizational structure can have a huge impact on how successful you are in your IT organization.

In our legacy organizations, most teams have been structured according to functional boundaries: the business analysis team, the project management office, the testing center of excellence, the development team, and the operations team. You could probably name a few more in your organization. However, this is not ideal, in part due to Conway's law, which says that your application architecture will reflect your organizational structure, most famously shortened to "If you have four groups working on a compiler, you'll get a four-pass compiler."[1]

The advent of Agile taught us about the power of colocation and how cross-functional teams can perform faster and more flexibly. In Agile, the ideal team has everyone in the team that needs to contribute to the success of a piece of work, from business analysis all the way to releasing it to production and supporting it in production. This sounds great, but I will be honest: I have never seen this in action. I work in large organizations where this is just not easily feasible—you would have to hire an exhibition hall to get all the people required into one room. However, there are ways to define organizational structures that get pretty close to the ideal cross-functional team, and they are achievable for just about any organization, no matter what size.

Lean and Agile thinking has also taught us the value of persistent teams. In the project-driven world, we run projects, which are finite by definition and for a specific purpose. As a result, in legacy organizations, once a project is completed, the team disbands, and the team members get assigned to new projects. In these new projects, the new team members have to learn the new context and have an *upskilling time* before they are as productive as they were before. We can avoid this delay by utilizing persistent teams who support a product or service, a change that might best be shortened from "building teams around work" to "bringing work to existing teams."

This change in approach requires a few organizational changes, the most difficult being that funding is often tied to projects. So, how can we get from funding projects to funding teams? There is no easy answer, unfortunately; and finding any answer tends to be difficult and context specific. A few pointers to help you with this task:

- Fund teams based on their value stream. SAFe provides a structure in which teams are funded based on the value stream they belong to.
- Get your business to agree to a funded team per budget cycle. I have worked with leaders who negotiated with business stakeholders to secure longer-term funding for a team.
- Hold back some funds to cover funding gaps. Some IT leaders I've worked with "charged" a slightly higher internal cost to make up for times when the team was not fully funded by projects.
- Creatively accrue funds based on the work the team is doing. The most committed product owners end up squirreling around the

organization to find pots of money between the proverbial sofa cushions, by doing work for several different stakeholders and hence getting access to those funds.

I don't think you will solve this problem quickly, but finding a few initial workarounds to start moving in this direction should be something on your to-do list. Measure the longevity of teams as one of your transformation metrics. Make it easy for the teams to stay together and become more productive together without losing context and becoming yet another silo.

Figure 6.1 shows the organizational structure that I recommend to clients as a good starting point to structuring their teams. I call it the "burger organization chart" due to the resemblance to a stylized burger. For the rest of the chapter, I walk you through the layers of the burger and explain from the bottom up how they work together successfully.

The Platform Team

There is a lot of controversy about whether or not having a DevOps team is the right thing to do. Some of the discussions are pretty evangelistic, and I personally prefer to look at results to make decisions, not at idealistic views of the world. If you attend the DevOps Enterprise Summit

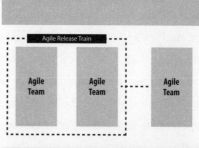

Figure 6.1:
Organizational structure starting point: This layered organizational structure works well in larger organizations

or other Agile or DevOps conferences, you will notice that organizations that made progress in their transformation efforts more often than not use a DevOps shared service, a DevOps team, or something similar. In the *2016 State of DevOps Report* from Puppet Labs, you will also see a lot of people self-identifying as part of a DevOps team; the proportion has increased from 2015 to 2016.[2] Roman Wilsenach calls the creation of a DevOps team an antipattern;[3] so, to avoid any confusion by the term "DevOps team," I just call it the platform team (feel free to call it the DevOps team in your organization—I won't be offended by the term). The platform team owns your development and run platform for your applications. In the end-state world, this development and run platform will act like an in-house-platform service provider that provides all your teams with self-service capabilities to support their delivery of solutions.*

Within this platform team, you will need to have people with skills across the whole set of DevOps capabilities. This means the team needs to cover infrastructure, configuration management, quality engineering, application deployment, monitoring, and release management, among others. As you can see, this is a team of cross-skilled experts, and I would expect some of your best engineers to be part of this team. Many organizations dealing with large legacy systems have structured themselves around technologies (e.g., a Windows team, a UNIX team, an Oracle team). The new platform team will still require some specialized skills for those technologies, but the focus will be a lot more on automation skills and the ability to redefine processes and architectures for the new world. As a result, you should not have technology-specific platform teams.

---

* For an interesting discussion on possible DevOps organizational structures, you can check out Matthew Skelton's blog post "What Team Structure Is Right for DevOps to Flourish?" The structure I represent here is close to type 4—the DevOps as a service model—in this case, for internal teams.[4]

We were working with an insurance company for which we were able to create a service catalog of this platform team across about a dozen different technology stacks (over forty services, such as application deployment and application compilation). For each service, we could then evaluate progress over time by looking at speed, reliability, and cost. This has proven very powerful to communicate some of the more technical improvements to business stakeholders.

The challenge I sometimes see with these platform teams is that they perceive themselves as "guardian" of DevOps rather than a service provider, and make it difficult for teams to adopt the platform. It is common to underestimate the level of change management required to make the adoption a success. When the platform is not able to support the teams in a way that makes life easier for teams, then those teams will look for alternatives to the common platform by creating their own custom solutions. A collaborative and flexible approach is required by the platform team to work with the teams they are providing the service for. Their platform should make doing the right thing easier than doing the wrong thing. It is also helpful to have some technical coaches in this team that have the capacity to sit with the teams when problems arise. Alternatively, you can rotate people between feature teams and the platform team or you can loan platform team members to feature teams, as this will help to break down cultural silos that might otherwise appear.

The platform team will evolve over time. When you initially form it, there will likely be many activities that require manual tasks, which means this team will be quite large; but it will shrink as more automation is introduced. To be able to introduce more and more automation over time, you will have to create sufficient capacity in the team to make the required improvements; otherwise, the old saying will become true: "We are too busy to help ourselves improve."

The accountabilities of the platform team include the following across development, test, and production environments:

- Software configuration management: this involves making sure all things required for the application are in version control.
- Application build process: The build scripts themselves are owned by the application team, but the execution and integration into the automation tool chain lie with the platform team. The build scripts are often jointly created to reflect requirements from the application and platform teams.
- Integration with test automation: Similarly, the test scripts are created by the application teams, but the execution is triggered from the platform. And results are reported by the platform team during scheduled runs.
- Environment provisioning: the teams collaborate in creating new environments and installing any required software.
- Application deployment: deploying the latest version or package of the application is also a joint effort.
- Monitoring: ongoing monitoring of infrastructure and applications is required across the environment landscape.
- Environment configuration management: make sure environments exist in the agreed configuration, identifying drift and correcting it where required.
- Reporting: this includes providing information about the health of the delivery platform and the performance of it.

You can see that it will take a while until you have a fully automated delivery platform, and managing the ongoing evolution of the platform team is a crucial aspect of your transformation. I am skeptical that this can be done as a big-bang project, as I have never seen anyone who could find a way around the number of unknowns and the speed of change in tools and technologies that can be leveraged. A structured roadmap and continuous improvement will create the best delivery platform for your organization.

One more tip from personal experience: the platform team needs to have change-management capability. Technical people tend to assume that once the right tools are in place, everyone will just follow the "right" process. This method usually fails. You need someone who is able to create trainings, run workshops, and deal with the users of the platform to understand the "experience" on the platform. I had a client who, after a workshop, said that they didn't need help with their DevOps transformation, because they had all the tools installed and it was just a matter of getting people to use those tools. Of course, the same client called again a few months later to discuss why their transformation had come off the rails. Take my advice and staff change-management people on the platform team. The engineers will love it, too, as they will get help with some of the required documentation they would otherwise have to do themselves.

Agile Teams

The "meat" of the burger is the Agile teams—where most of the work is being done. For this book, I will ignore the fact that some of the delivery teams will be Waterfall project teams that continue to work in a traditional way (there is a lot of literature out there telling you how to deliver well with traditional teams). Instead, I will highlight the Agile-focused delivery teams, as this route requires changes to your organization.

Let's start by discussing the composition of these teams. A lot has been said about cross-skilled teams and bringing operations people into the teams to achieve DevOps, in effect adding more and more people with specialist skills to an ever-increasing team. For me, just bringing more and more people into the same team is all too simplistic, as it does not scale well in complex environments where many different skills across Dev and Ops are required to achieve an outcome. Rather than bloating the team by adding people, we need to focus teams on building the product and, in this process, consuming services from other teams that are nondifferentiating, like application deployments. The Agile teams should have a product owner, business analysts, a Scrum master, developers, quality engineers, and testers in the proportions that are required to design, build, and test the system. Over time, each team member should build skills across multiple dimensions, aiming for a T-shaped skill profile.[†] We will let the platform team deal with how the application gets deployed and how the environment needs to look for the application to run well. The Agile teams will collaborate with the platform team, but they don't need to have a full-time DevOps engineer in their team; when more support is required, a DevOps engineer can be loaned to the Agile team as required, full-time or part-time.

Furthermore, in most organizations there will be an external testing team to support later phases of testing. The accountability of the Agile teams is really to get the system into a state that it is as close to releasable as possible. For this to be efficient, the Agile team will use definitions of ready to determine when a user story can be used for delivery and has sufficient detail to become part of the sprint backlog. It uses a definition of done to determine when all activities that can be completed during a sprint/iteration are completed. Typical definitions of ready include the following: story has been sized, wireframes have been agreed, acceptance criteria and test cases have been defined. Definitions of done should, at minimum, include the following: code has been developed, functionality has been documented, story has been tested at unit and application level, and product owner or delegate has seen and accepted the story.

From a DevOps perspective, the Agile teams should be responsible not just for delivery of new functionality but also for fixing any production defects or minor changes coming from production. The teams are responsible for the application they are building and are not handing it off

---

[†] T-shaped people have a working understanding of many areas and are deeply specialized in one of them (compared to I-shaped people, who know only one area). See the appendix for details.

to some other "production team" or "fix team." This changes the incentive for good code and maintainability of the application significantly.

This shift in end-to-end responsibility means that Agile teams should be meaningfully aligned to business processes. The best way to do this is by having one or more Agile teams supporting a value stream in your business. Large organizations will need more than one Agile team to support their business value streams, which is where the SAFe concept of *release trains* comes in to orchestrate and manage a group of Agile teams to support a value stream.‡ Within this group of Agile teams, the technical composition of those Agile teams requires some consideration.

Ideally, you want to have Agile feature teams that can deliver functionality independently. Those Agile feature teams have developers from all the impacted applications and can develop across system boundaries. This works better when all the developers are from the same organization and are in the same location. As you start using more than one system integrator in multiple locations, I believe this model breaks down, as it requires too much orchestration within the same Agile feature team, and the distributed nature makes it difficult to develop a common team culture across organizational boundaries.

If you are working with multiple vendors, you can use Agile feature teams successfully if you can colocate them in the same premises, as colocation usually overrides cultural differences over time. Or you might want to explore a captive model offshore. In captive models, your vendors work on your premises under your direction, which gives you more control over the work methods and culture of your delivery teams.

If you are working with only one vendor as strategic partner, then you can make a distributed, multitechnology Agile feature team successful, as there is some cohesion due to the organizational guidance between the

---

‡ You can read more about release trains on ScaledAgileFramework.com.

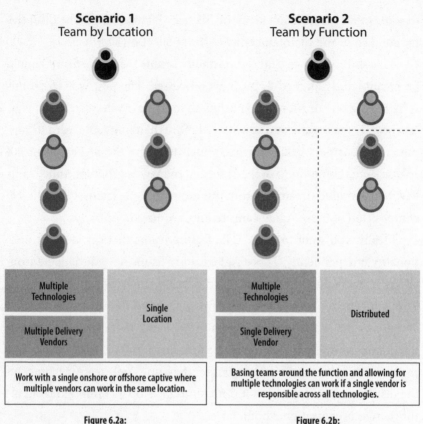

Scenario 1
Team by Location

Scenario 2
Team by Function

Multiple Technologies		Single Location
Multiple Delivery Vendors		

Work with a single onshore or offshore captive where multiple vendors can work in the same location.

Multiple Technologies		Distributed
Single Delivery Vendor		

Basing teams around the function and allowing for multiple technologies can work if a single vendor is responsible across all technologies.

Figure 6.2a:
Agile team scenario 1: Agile feature teams in one location can be from multiple vendors and support multiple technologies

Figure 6.2b:
Agile team scenario 2: Distributed Agile feature teams ideally consist of one vendor only

two organizations. Having both multivendor and multitechnology in a distributed Agile feature team is extremely difficult in my experience.

The alternative team model is to define Agile component teams along application or technology boundaries. This is the best approach for multivendor, multilocation models. It requires more cross-team orchestration, but this can be achieved through common planning and synchronization events like the PI planning and systems demo in SAFe. While this is not the ideal model, from my delivery experience, this model is far easier to manage in the multivendor, multilocation scenario.

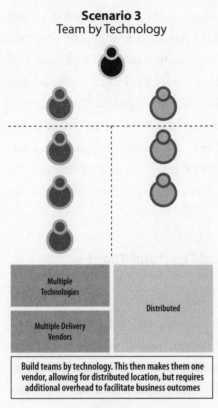

Scenario 3
Team by Technology

Multiple
Technologies

Multiple Delivery
Vendors

Distributed

Build teams by technology. This then makes them one vendor, allowing for distributed location, but requires additional overhead to facilitate business outcomes

Figure 6.2c:
Agile team scenario 3: Agile component teams in multi vendor, multi location scenarios

I want to offer one last comment on team structure before we move on to test automation. Colocation versus distribution, in my experience, is a balance between flexibility/speed (having the team colocated with your business) and cost (having more members of your team offshore). You will have to decide what is more important for your organization. All things being equal, distributed teams carry higher management cost and require more time for delivery, but high-performing distributed teams still beat the average colocated team on both dimensions. Your context and your knowledge of the teams should guide you here.

Test Automation Center

Test automation initiatives are the DevOps-related capability that I see fail more often than any other initiative, yet they are a very important prerequisite for many of the things we want to achieve to maintain high-quality outcomes. In the high-level organizational structure, I put in a test automation center as a transitionary state. I believe that most organizations will need the center to have someone with a dedicated focus on making test automation work and to create the overall test automation framework. This is the scope of the test automation center, which is staffed by test architects and test automation engineers who own the test automation framework. Over time, this function and team will disperse, and test automation will be supported by the test engineers and architects within the application team. They are supported by a dynamic community of practice where the test automation framework is being maintained in an open-source fashion. Of course, organizations can choose to make this team a permanent fixture. Given that this team is much smaller in comparison to traditional testing centers of excellence, it is also a lot cheaper.

The Governance and Coaching Team

I spoke earlier about defining Lean governance processes for your organization that rely on objective measures and not subjective concepts. Naturally, this governance needs to have a "home," which is what this governance and coaching team represents. At the beginning of the transformation, when your rate of transformational change is still high, this team is a bit larger, as it also contains your organizational coaches, your Agile coaches, and a transformation governance function, which all reduce as the rate of change reduces. Let's talk about the different aspects of governance that are required to be covered by this team.

Architecture Governance

It is an unspoken secret that your application architecture will be the determinant factor on how fast you are able to deliver. Architecture governance has, therefore, three main purposes:

1. to ensure that each initiative continues to decouple the application architecture further, making it more flexible by creating

flexible interfaces between applications and by following a modular application architecture paradigm;

2. to make sure each initiative reduces the overall technical debt in the systems; and

3. to monitor the evolution of the application architecture, making sure it evolves in line with the company vision and that the applications continue to support the business appropriately. (We will come back later to the ways architecture can evolve.)

It is important to mention that architecture governance needs to be done in close collaboration with the application teams to avoid creating an ivory tower function that is prescribing ideals that are beyond practicality.

Method Governance

There are many different delivery methods available to organizations these days. The method governance function makes sure that the most appropriate method is being used for each initiative. It also engages with teams to coach them in how to apply those methods and how to maintain the company's internal definition of the methods to provide a common framework for everyone to use. I have learned from my engagements that a proliferation of terminology and practices without common framework leads to friction as you adopt and scale Agile methods.

Delivery-Quality Governance

Speed to market is our key goal, yet doing this without the right quality defeats the purpose. The delivery-quality governance function looks at measures across the SDLC to identify where quality concerns arise and how to improve the overall delivery quality without impacting speed or cost of delivery in the long run.

Continuous-Improvement Governance

As mentioned before, a rigorous continuous-improvement governance function is key to the overall transformation. For each larger initiative, this function will support the definition of success measures, the baselining of those measures, and the evaluation of success afterward. It will also be the owner/manager of the continuous-improvement funding who supports the most promising improvement initiatives following a weighted shortest job first (WSJF) approach. Under a WSJF prioritization, initiatives of similar benefit are prioritized by size. The smaller they are, the higher they will be prioritized, hence making sure that feedback cycles are as fast as possible.[5]

But Wait—What Happened to Project Managers?

You might wonder why my organizational structure does not have a project management office and why I don't mention project managers in the team section. I am not in the camp of people who believe project managers are a thing of the past. I think there is a good reason to have project managers. In this structure of persistent teams, however, the project managers don't really fit in. By definition, a project is something that exists for a specific period of time to achieve a specific outcome. As such, project managers will be responsible for managing the delivery of projects through the team structure indicated. There should be a lot fewer projects in this end state as the work flows toward teams as Agile work items (epics, features, or stories), which means you will have fewer project managers. But for large, complex projects, you might employ a project manager to manage delivery across the teams and to report on all the work specific to the project—something that might otherwise be difficult to get out of the delivery teams who are working more holistically on the backlog. The role of the project manager should therefore be a more active and involved role that goes beyond the management of project plans and includes active contribution to the Agile planning events as stakeholder.

First Steps for Your Organization

Identify One of Your Value Streams and the Required Teams to Support It

We have spoken about creating a value stream map before (in chapter 2). What we are looking for here is to identify value streams from a business perspective. Once you have identified the value stream, the next step is to identify the systems that support the value stream.

Looking at your backlog of work or your portfolio of initiatives, identify how much work impacts the systems supporting this value stream. On this basis, you should now be able to create a team structure supporting this value stream. It won't be perfect, and you will have to adjust it over time; but you now have a starting point. Using the SAFe terminology, you have identified an Agile release train, and you can now go on to deliver work through this team structure to support the value stream. Over time, you will be able to shift the budgeting model to support the teams as I mentioned earlier in the chapter.

Identify the Teams That Will Be Impacted by the Move to a Platform Team

The platform team is a concept that is very transformational, and the change required is often underestimated. To help you navigate this change, I want you to identify all the teams that are currently performing functions that would ultimately be performed by the platform team or would be impacted by the platform team (e.g., infrastructure teams, testing teams, database administrators [DBAs]). Invite them to a workshop to discuss what the delivery platform at your organization should look like from a functional perspective. Once you have a level of agreement on that, discuss how the delivery platform should be supported. Hopefully the platform team emerges as something that everyone can agree on. Then agree on next steps to get closer to achieving this end-state vision.

CHAPTER 7

From Testers to Quality Engineers

Good testers are people who look both ways
before crossing a one-way street.

—**Common testing saying**

In the last chapter, I talked about the organizational structure of your IT transformation, and my "burger chart" of an appropriate organizational structure (Figure 6.1) had aspects of testing included. Why do I spend another separate chapter on testing? In my experience, the organizational change associated with testing is by far the most significant and the one that organizations struggle with the most. The change journey for people in testing roles is even greater—a role that used to be focused on execution of test scripts but has evolved into either a very technical test engineer role or into business experts who evaluate risks and then design a test strategy around them. Every day, I see clients who still prefer separate test organizations focusing on traditional manual testing (which is often highly dysfunctional and optimized for cost instead of speed or risk) and would like us to help build these. More often than not, I see failed or suboptimal test automation initiatives by clients who are driven by those test organizations and test managers. The change from traditional testing to quality engineering will require a mind-set shift in the people who work in testing. Not everyone will be able to make that transition. While this chapter focuses on the organizational dimension, I will expand on technical topics as required to illustrate the point.

The Quality Organization

Quality is such an important aspect that is reflected in all parts of the organization. At the top of Figure 6.1, in the governance layer, the standards and principles are defined that play a large role to ensure quality. You will also need to look at the day-to-day quality as shown in the actual software you deliver, which should be part of your governance. This means your measures of quality and the outputs from retrospectives and reviews need to be discussed to identify where the overall quality process can be improved and where standards need to be adjusted.

Initially, the test automation team is required to set up the test automation framework and to work with the platform team to build the right integrations that allow for targeted automation runs (e.g., just functionality that was impacted). This team's primary job is to enable all the test engineers to leverage the test automation framework successfully; hence, a lot of coaching and pair programming is required to help make the quality engineers familiar with the framework. The team also needs to provide guardrails so that the overall test automation is not failing in the long run. Those guardrails ensure that test execution does not take too long or require too many resources, for example—both common problems of test automation frameworks that grow over time. Guardrails can be coding standards, common libraries, regular peer reviews, or other technical documentation and governance processes. In the early days, this will be pretty intense, especially as the test automation framework evolves to support all the data flows. Later on, this team can reduce in size when the test engineers become familiar with the framework and don't require as much support. While my clients tend to make the test automation team a permanent fixture, I can imagine this function disappearing completely as a separate team and just being picked up by the more experienced test engineers.

We spoke about the platform team before. Just to recap, this team will integrate the scripts so that the overall pipeline enforces good behavior and makes the results visible. The platform team also works with the test engineers to agree on standards that will make sure the scripts work on the platform (e.g., for environment variables).

And then, of course, the test engineers in the delivery teams have ownership of the test automation scripts and make sure all functional areas are covered. They work with all other teams, as they are end-to-end accountable for the quality of the service.

The Quality Engineering Process

Let's look at a common misconception: test automation is just the automation of tests you would otherwise run manually. This is not true. This is probably the number-one reason why test automation initiatives fail: they try to automate the kind of testing that they have traditionally done manually. In rare cases this might work, but more often, this approach will fail. I like the term "quality engineering" a lot more than test automation because it avoids the term "test," which many associate with the last-ditch effort to find all the bugs at the end of the SDLC. Quality engineering speaks to the end-to-end aspect of automation to ensure a quality product at the end. This means that the person or team responsible for quality engineering needs to look at the full life cycle and not just the testing phase—a shift that is quite challenging. Test automation (e.g., the automated execution of test scripts) is an activity within quality engineering.

The traditional testing center of excellence was set up as an antagonist to the delivery team, who controls the quality of delivery by mass inspection. This created dysfunction, as a lot of opportunities for quality improvements were missed, and often, the teams would argue about who was accountable for the product's lack of quality (the testers for not finding the problems or the developers for creating them). It's quite easy to put yourself in the shoes of the developers and say, "It's okay if there is a problem; it's the testers' job to find them." On the flip side, a tester could say, "I should be able to take it easy, as a good developer would not create defects in the first place." You want to break this dynamic by making quality a common goal. Deming said that "quality comes not from inspection but from improvement of the production process."[1] This means that testers who take this to heart will start playing a more involved role in the delivery process, not as antagonist but, rather, as a member of the team.

Another thing that has gone wrong is the way we measure quality—many organizations use defects or *defect density* as a measure. Measuring increased quality through the number of defects does not give any good indication of overall quality.* You agree, I hope, that we need better ways

---

* I am very skeptical of number of defects as a quality metric. I was talking to a company in the United States who had gone through an IT improvement program because they had so many defects in their SDLC. After they told the IT department that number of defects is the key metric, the number of defects quickly reduced. When the number of defects reached a low point, the organization considered ramping down the testing function as quality was not a concern anymore. Yet before they could finalize such a decision, the number of defects started increasing again. The transformation lead called both the delivery team lead and the testing lead into his office and asked for an explanation of this pattern. The answer was obvious in hindsight: when defect was the key metric for development, the development team worked very closely with the testing team to make sure that functionality was "pretested" before the formal test, and any concerns were quickly rectified. They even introduced a new ticket type in their defect tracking system called "predefect query." Once the testing department heard rumors that they would be downsized because of the increased quality level, they started to raise more defects and fewer "predefect queries." The IT transformation lead told me that at this point, he realized the inherent quality in the delivery process itself had not changed at all during his program and that all the change was in the support process.

to improve quality, so let's discuss what can be done meaningfully and how we will measure this.

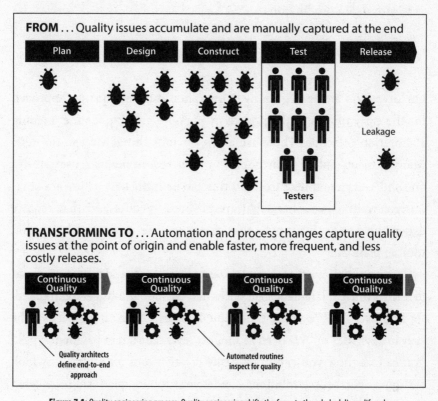

Figure 7.1: Quality engineering process: Quality engineering shifts the focus to the whole delivery lifecycle

Quality engineering is leveraging the idea that you should build quality in whatever you do and look for ways to do more testing without additional cost (in both money and time). Frameworks like SAFe and disciplined Agile delivery (DAD) have made this one of their principles. What does this mean in practice, though? Let's break down the process into five phases:

1. requirements, design, and architecture
2. coding

3. Agile testing
4. hardening
5. running in production

Requirements, Design, and Architecture

Quality starts at the beginning, so we should have a quality approach for the early phases of the project or in Agile projects for the ongoing elaboration of scope. There are a few obvious things we can do here. Many projects suffer from poorly written requirements / user stories and short-term architectures. But this can be mitigated. There are obviously certain aspects here that are business specific and that require experts to be involved, but other things can be supported by a good tooling platform.

Accenture uses a tool that analyzes requirements and user stories, and identifies unclear language. Sentences that are ambiguous get highlighted: for example, "The response time should be *fast*," "The screen needs to be *easy to navigate*," or "We need to support *several* different payment types." You can see how you can quite easily create a tool for yourself or look for some open source solutions that let your tooling platform learn what unclear language is. With the introduction of more and more artificial intelligence into the IT life cycle, you might soon see products that go beyond key-word recognition.

On the architecture side, there is a qualitative aspect that your architects need to be involved with. They should make sure that each initiative is leaving your architecture in a better place than it was found. *Decoupling of systems* and modules needs to be one of the core aspects they encourage. As discussed before, there is no end-state architecture anymore that architects need to define and try to enforce; they just need to help make the architecture fluid and flexible for the future so that continuous evolution is possible and gets easier over time, not harder.

Traditional approaches accrued technical debt in the architecture, and changes became increasingly expensive. Hence, the performance of your architects should be evaluated on how flexible the architecture is becoming. For example, how do the architects make sure your architecture is future proof? There are some aspects of architecture that you can measure, and I encourage you to find these measures so that you have something to help drive the right behavior: number of database access requests, data volume transferred over interfaces, *stateless calls* versus *stateful calls*, number of calls to external systems, response and CPU times. As trends over time, these give you interesting and useful information about the maturity of your architecture.

An important part of architecture governance is having a set of clearly defined architecture principles. Everyone in your organization should know what architecture means in your context. You don't have to go as far as Amazon (where an anecdote says that Jeff Bezos made it a mandate to use service orientation at the threat of being fired otherwise),[2] but having an opinionated view for your organization is important to align all the moving parts. As you can see, we are trying to create collaboration and accountability across the whole life cycle of delivery; we are breaking the functional silos, not by restructuring but by overlapping accountabilities.

Coding

The quality aspects of coding are usually undervalued. I have talked to many organizations, and very few know or care about what quality measures are taken in the coding phase, instead relying on the testing phase. When working with system integrators, there is often disagreement on the quality measures during coding. But there are a few things that should be mandatory: static code analysis, automated unit-testing, and peer reviews. You should have an automated unit-testing framework that is being used to test modules directly by the developer in an automated fashion. They are available for many technologies, like jUnit for Java or nUnit for .NET—there is really no excuse for not using this and letting your developers get away with some level of manual testing. Additionally, static code analysis is quite easy to implement, even for technologies like COTS packages. Your coding standards can, to a large degree, be codified and enforced through this.

The manual peer review of code that many organizations use (although often in a terribly inefficient way) should only happen after the automated static code analysis and unit tests have been run. You don't want to waste expensive and time-consuming manual effort on things that automation can address for you. Peer reviews should focus on architectural and conceptual aspects of the code, as well as fit-for-purpose (e.g., does this piece of code solve the problem?).

I have been in organizations that have, over time, added to their peer-review checklist new items whenever a problem was found. This meant the checklist had over 150 items at some stage. Guess what? No one was actually following that checklist anymore because it was too long, and too much was irrelevant on a day-by-day basis. Create a simple and short checklist as a guide, and teach people what to look for by pairing them up with experienced developers during the peer-review process.

You can also get a group of developers together on a regular basis to peer review some selected changes as a group, so that they can learn from each other and align on the coding style in the team. And make code review easy by supporting it with proper tooling that shows the actual changed lines of code and reason for the change. Don't make the peer-review process cumbersome by asking the reviewer to find the changes in the code herself and fill in Excel sheets for feedback. That does not help anyone. Get her to provide feedback directly, in context of the user story and in the same work management system that everyone uses.

Agile Testing

It does not matter whether you formally use an Agile method or not; the best way to do functional testing is to have the testers and developers sit together. The test engineers should be writing the test automation code in parallel with the developers writing the functional code. When the two functions work together, it is much easier to write testable code that can be automated. This is one of the critical aspects to make test automation successful and affordable.

If you have a test automation team that owns the framework, the test engineers will leverage this during development, providing feedback to the framework team. Additionally, the test engineers will work with the tooling platform team to integrate the right test scripts, so that during the automated build and deploy process, only the required scripts are executed. We are aiming for fast feedback here, not for full coverage. We can do a full run off-cycle on a weekend or overnight.

During development, we also want to check for performance and security concerns. While this might not be exactly the same as in production or preproduction environments due to environment constraints, we are happy to accept the fast feedback we get as indication. We actually prefer speed over accuracy. If we can find defects 70% of the time earlier in the life cycle and find the other 30% in the later phases, where we would normally find them, then that is actually fine. Remember: we are automating all aspects of quality checks, so we can run them a lot more frequently. From a performance perspective, we might not have accurate performance results; but if an action is becoming slower over time, we know we have something to look at that indicates a possible problem later on.

This fast feedback allows the developer to try different approaches to tune performance while he still has the context instead of weeks later, when the final performance testing fails and the developer has built a whole solution on top of his first design idea. The same is true for security testing: take the early feedback wherever you can get it.

Hardening

As much as I wish that all testing could be done within the Agile team, it is often not possible due to a number of factors. We therefore introduce a hardening phase to run tests involving external systems, time-consuming batch runs, and security testing by a third party. This hardening happens right before going to production. I personally think that you want to do some testing with the business users in a user-acceptance testing activity as well, which cannot be automated. You don't want your business stakeholder to test based on the test cases already performed but for usability and fit-for-purpose.

Running in Production

I won't spend much time here, as I will talk about keeping a system running in a later chapter, but it should be clear that certain quality assurance activities should happen for the service in production. You want to monitor your servers and services, but you also want to look for performance, availability, and functional accuracy concerns in production. All of this should still be part of the overall quality plan.

A Few Words on Functional Test Automation

As I said before, test automation is the one DevOps-related activity that tends to challenge organizations, requiring a real mind-set shift in the people involved. However, I have seen a few common failure patterns that I want to share with you so that you can avoid repeating them in your organization.

Don't Underestimate the Impact on Infrastructure and the Ecosystem

There is a physical limit to how much pressure a number of manual testers can put on your systems; automation puts very different stress on your system. What you otherwise do once a week manually you might now do a hundred times a day with automation. Add into the mix an integrated environment, and your external systems need to respond more frequently too. So, you really have to consider two different aspects: Can your infrastructure in your environments support a hundred times the volume it currently supports? And are your external systems set up to support this volume? Of course, you can always choose to reduce the stress on external systems by limiting the real-time interactions and stub out a certain percentage of transactions, or you can use virtual services.

Don't Underestimate the Data Hunger

Very often, automated test scripts are used in the same environment where manual testing takes place. Test automation is data hungry, as it needs data for each run of test execution; and remember, this is happening much more frequently than the manual testing does. Therefore, you cannot easily refresh all test data whenever you want to run your automated scripts, as manual testing might still be in progress; you will have to wait until manual testing reaches a logical refresh point. This obviously is not good enough for multiple reasons; instead, you need to be able to run your test automation at any time. Fortunately, there are a few different strategies you can use to remedy the situation (and you will likely use a combination):

- Finish the test in the same state of data that you started with.
- Create the data as part of the test execution.

- Identify a partial set of data across all involved applications that you can safely replace each time.
- Leverage a large base of data sets to feed into your automation to last until the next logical refresh point.

Consider the Whole System, Not One Application

Test automation is often an orchestration exercise, as the overall business process in testing flows across many different applications. If you require manual steps in multiple systems, then your automation will depend on orchestrating all of those. By just building automation for one system, you might get stuck if your test automation solution is not able to be orchestrated across different solutions. Also, some *walled-garden test automation tools* might not play well together, so think about your overall system of applications and the business processes first before heavily investing in one specific solution for one application.

Not Following the Test Automation Pyramid

Automating testing should follow the test automation pyramid (Figure 7.2). Most tests should be fast-executing unit tests at component level. The heavy lifting is done in the service or functional layer, where we test through APIs and only a few tests are run through the user interface (UI). When considering manual testing, you usually need to work through the UI. Many test automation approaches try to emulate this by automating the same test cases through the UI. The reality is that the UI is slow and brittle. You want to refactor your testing approach to leverage the service layer instead; otherwise, you will pay for it by increasing amounts of rework of your automated test scripts.

Test automation for legacy applications is a tricky business. You have so much functionality to cover, and it tends to not be economical to do

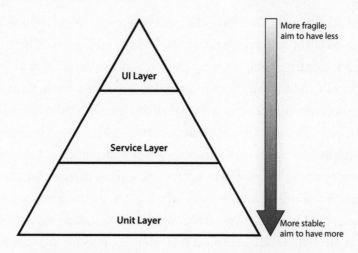

Figure 7.2: Test automation pyramid: The slower the layer, the less we should use it in automating tests

that as a big bang. My advice is to start with a small set of regression tests for your legacy applications so that you can ensure the quality of the application for the higher-priority functionality. Then use changes to the application or areas for which you perform *refactoring* to build additional test cases. In the case of new functionality being built, get the set of new test cases built with the code changes. In the cases of *refactoring*, build the test case first, make sure it works and passes with the current application, and then, after refactoring, it should still work.[†]

Quality Management and Measurements

As I said earlier in this chapter, you will have to find overall measures for quality outcome and quality process. Measure how well your process is working to identify quality concerns automatically, and measure how fast

---

[†] At the DevOps Enterprise Forum in 2015, a group created some guidance about test automation for legacy application. The paper, *Tactics for Implementing Test Automation for Legacy Code*, is worth reading if you want to learn more.[3]

and accurate it is. One thing that makes people stumble is when the automation is not well maintained; these process measures will help you keep that in control. Look for measures such as the duration of your regression run and the false positives coming from your test automation. The quality outcome measure should really be based on production incidents and perhaps defects found in the hardening phase. Don't measure defects the delivery team finds itself, as the team is meant to find as many problems as possible. Documenting and measuring defects that the delivery team is finding themselves is of little benefit; let the team focus on finding and addressing them. Only when defects escape the delivery team into later phases do you need documentation to manage the handover between teams.

A helpful way to embed this into your teams is by using differentiated terminology to distinguish the phase the problem has been found in. I like to use *bug*, *defect*, and *incident*. A bug is something the Agile team finds that prevents the story from being accepted by the product owner. In this case, there is no formal documentation; rather, the tester provides as much information as possible to the developer to fix the bug. Once the bug has been fixed, the story gets tested again, and the process repeats until the product owner can accept the story. We don't measure bugs in any formal way. Once another team gets involved, like the hardening team, then we call problems *defects* and manage them with a defect life cycle, and we can measure how many defects "escape" from the Agile team. These defects can be used to analyse what limitations prevent the Agile team from finding them themselves and helps them to design countermeasures. In production, we call problems with the code *incidents*, and those are the quality concerns that we absolutely want to measure, as they impact our customers. Incidents are the ultimate quality measure of our product or service.

Then there are the production run metrics like uptime and functional availability, but we will cover this in the chapter about application management (chapter 11).

First Steps for Your Organization

Mapping the Quality Process of Your Organization

This activity is somewhat similar to the value mapping we did in chapter 1. Here again, you should prepare a whiteboard or other wall space, and be ready with Blu Tack and system cards.

First, create a high-level work flow on the wall, showing requirements to production, including all the relevant process steps represented on the cards. Then use a different color of cards or pen and list each quality activity where it happens in the life cycle.

To make sure the picture is complete, ask yourself whether you have covered all concerns, including performance, security, availability, and any other concerns. It's okay if you have some aspects missing from the original list; simply highlight these on the side.

As a next step, your team needs to think about automation: What can be automated and hence be done earlier and more frequently? Consider breaking up activities into an automated part that can be completed earlier and more frequently, as well as a part that continues to require a manual inspection. Remember that automated activities are nearly free of effort once implemented, so doing them more often does not add much cost.

Now, you want to identify opportunities to check for quality aspects earlier, as this relates to manual inspection. For each activity think of possible ways to do the full scope or at least aspects of it earlier.

Finally, create a backlog in which your teams can make the required shifts toward quality engineering, and then start making the shift.

Measuring Quality

As discussed in this chapter, measuring quality is not easy. Many measures are only valid temporarily, while you are addressing specific concerns. Sit down with your quality or testing leadership and, on a piece of paper, list out at all the metrics and measures you use to determine quality. Then determine which ones are objective and automated.

If you don't have a good set of automated and objective metrics, then workshop how to get to a small set of these. I think two of the easy ones to agree on are duration for a successful regression test run and incidents found in production per time period. These are pretty noncontroversial and applicable to all kinds of companies, but you will want to define a small number of additional metrics relevant to your business.

CHAPTER 8

Managing People, Not Resources

> Managing teams would be easy if it wasn't for
> the people you have to deal with.
> —**Anonymous** (my first supervisor)

Some people react allergically when you call people resources and talk about managing resources. While not exactly allergic, I agree with the underlying sentiment. A resource is something you can manage without much tailoring; you can treat one bag of sand like the next bag of sand when it comes to making dikes. With people, that is never true. We have probably all been planning for projects and creating a plan that includes a certain amount of "anonymous full-time equivalents (FTEs)." Then a bit later, we start putting names to it and realize that we need more or less effort based on the actual people we have available for the project. One Java developer is just not the same as another; and honestly, we would never consider ourselves to be just a resource whose job someone else could do with the same efficiency and effectiveness. So, why do we then pretend that we can manage our people like anonymous resources?

For me, it comes back to that legacy thinking inspired by manufacturing, where replacing a worker on the assembly line was actually much easier than it would be today to replace a Java developer. In this chapter,

I will provide some guidance on how to approach management using humanistic practices.* The beauty of this chapter is that the approach is valid across the organization, from the first line manager all the way up to the CIO. And after all, the way people are being managed in your organization has a huge influence on your culture. So, getting this right, setting the right example, and encouraging the people who work for you to follow the same can make a real difference.

When I just started working after university, I saw a few things in the organization I was working for that I really didn't like—the way certain things were handled. My boss, who had a very open mind and an open-door policy, allowed me to vent and then provided one of the best pieces of advice in my career: "Mirco, you will not be able to get the organization to change, but what you can do is change your part of the organization. Once you are a manager, manage your teams the way that you would like to be treated, and then get results. As you climb higher in the hierarchy, your area of influence will increase and, with that, a larger and larger part of the organization will work the way you would like it to. It will be hard, but who knows? One day you may be at the top and will have only yourself to blame for the culture you have created along the way."[1] I am still pretty far away from the top, but his guidance has stayed with me throughout my career.

What I am writing about in this chapter is the way I try to operate as well. Those readers who have worked for me or are still working for me will know that I am far from perfect and that I use these practices myself whenever possible. Becoming a better people manager is a never-ending job.

---

* If you are familiar with Mark Horstman and Michael Auzanne over at Manager-Tools. com, then you will find quite a bit of material inspired by them in this chapter. Their podcast and their conferences (which is what they call their trainings) are some of the best guidance on management that is out there. The podcasts are free, and the conferences are very affordable and available around the world. Give them a try.

One-On-Ones

The first practice that I want you all to do (if you are not doing it already) is to have regular one-on-one meetings with the people who report directly to you. It's very hard to manage someone as a person when she is just an anonymous entity that you only know through her work product. And no, having an open-door policy is not the same as setting up one-on-ones. With an open-door policy, your directs might still feel that they are imposing themselves on you, and the resulting meetings might have less structure than you would like them to have. Your setting up the meetings and following through sends the sign that your people are important to you and that you are making time for them.

A weekly or biweekly thirty-minute slot works out very well. You want to use this meeting to learn more about the person over time, without it feeling like an interrogation. Always give the direct the first part of the meeting to raise anything she has to say or ask, and then provide your updates and information that could be important for her afterward. Once you start doing one-on-ones, you will see that after a while, the direct comes prepared with her items and that you get a lot fewer requests for ad hoc meetings. One-on-ones not only provide you with the opportunity to get to know the person, they will also make you more effective as a manager, increasing the time you have to focus on your job. This is possible because the people who work for you won't disrupt you during the week with nonurgent queries, as they know they have time within each week (or every other week) when they can receive guidance on all of those things.

In my experience, you should not skip more than one in four, or 25%, of the one-on-ones for them to be meaningful and positively impact your relationship with your directs and their results. Everyone I know loves one-on-ones after doing them for a while, so stick with them for at least two months before you judge them.† Many of the people I have had one-on-ones with went off and introduced them to the teams they work with, which is a great endorsement of the practice.

Feedback

Just about everyone I know would like to get more feedback from his or her boss, yet as bosses, we are often uncomfortable giving feedback (especially the constructive kind that requires behavior adjustment; positive feedback is somewhat easier). If you think about it, you probably learn the most from constructive feedback, but it is a bit uncomfortable to give. Plus, there are good ways to give feedback, and there are bad ways. I come back to Dan Pink's mastery, autonomy, and purpose;[2] you want to motivate the direct to improve by appealing to all three aspects.

Your feedback should focus on concrete situations that are recent, not generalizations such as "you are often late" or "your work product is not of good quality." It should describe the impact the behavior had and should ask for a change in behavior. An example: "When you don't use an agenda for a meeting like you did this morning with our vendor, we spend a lot of time discussing with no clear outcome in mind, and don't achieve a result. Could you do this differently next time?"

You can see that this example is timely (from a meeting the same morning), it shows why you want the behavior to change to increase mastery of the skill in question, and it leaves the direct with the autonomy to decide the next steps to improve. Of course, the direct can ask for further guidance, but this simple feedback model works in line with Dan Pink's motivators.

---

† There is a lot of guidance on one-on-ones on the Manager Tools website including introduction emails and a series of podcasts on how to run them well. If you have specific challenges with them, check Manager Tools for this as well; it has plenty of good advice on how to tweak the one-on-one for specific circumstances.

I use this template, which keeps me focused on the key elements of feedback (behavior, consequence, and the need to change): When you do x, y happens, which is not optimal. Can you find a way to do it differently next time to lead to a better outcome?

You can use the same template for positive feedback. In this case, you obviously don't ask for a change but rather for the direct to continue doing the same. This kind of positive feedback appeals to the three motivators a lot more than a "good job" or "you did well."

Delegation

When I started as a manager, I felt bad delegating work that I could do myself or that was not terribly rewarding (e.g., filling in forms). Listening to the podcast *Manager Tools*, I learned of a concept called "Managerial Economics 101,"[3] which means that if the same task can be done by someone with a lower cost rate, then it is uneconomic to not delegate it. Understanding this changed my life as a manager, as I started to feel less bad about delegating such work to people who work for me. On the flip side, I also started to think more about tasks that my boss might not have delegated because she felt bad, and I volunteered myself to help her out. Trust me, she was very thankful for me picking up those tasks. Keeping this in mind can get you a lot of positive credit with your boss.

The key to making delegation meaningful for the employee is to use the three motivators during the delegation process. Explain how the tasks will help the direct learn something new, how it helps you as a manager to do your job better, and after the initial handover, let the direct determine the best way to do it as long as the outcome is correct.

An example could be: "Michael, could you please help me by doing the weekly status reporting going forward? When you take care of this for me, I can focus on preparing the key messages for the meeting, which allows me to present the progress of our project much better to our stakeholders.

The reports need to follow our standard template for status. I am happy to show you how I did it in the past, but I will leave it to you to determine the best way going forward. I am happy to do the report together for the first couple of times. Do you have any questions about the task?"

Creating a Blameless Culture

As a boss, your job is to protect the individuals in your team from outside criticism. When a problem occurs in your team, you will have to cover it without delegating the blame to the person in your team who is responsible. The team will appreciate this. For praise, the opposite is true: the more you share with the rest of the organization the positive impact a member of your team has made, the better you will look too. These two practices empower the people on your team to do the best job they can for you. And the rest of the organization will always hold you accountable for the results of your team anyway, so pushing blame further down or withholding praise actually does nothing positive for you.

This is the other aspect of management that is worth highlighting—creating a blameless culture. If you think back to the argument I made about the system being responsible for the behavior of people, it becomes clear that for any mistakes, the system is more to blame than the individual employee. Etsy goes so far as to make each engineer deploy to production on his or her first day on the job. After all, if the new engineer can break production, the system is clearly not good enough to withstand simple mistakes.[4] So, whenever you have failures or problems, your root-cause analysis should not focus on who did what but on how we need to change the system so that the next person is able to avoid making the mistake again. Combining this kind of post-incident behavior within your team—with the protection from blame from the outside, as mentioned before—will start shifting the culture of your team to a more positive and empowering environment where they can thrive and achieve the best results for the organization. But how do you measure this culture to see whether it is improving?

Measuring Your Organizational Culture

There are a few different ways to measure culture. One that we highlighted in the DevOps metrics paper *Measure Efficiency, Effectiveness, and Culture to Optimize DevOps Transformation*, is the Westrum survey measures:

- On my team, information is actively sought.
- On my team, failures are learning opportunities, and messengers of them are not punished.
- On my team, responsibilities are shared.
- On my team, cross-functional collaboration is encouraged and rewarded.
- On my team, failure causes inquiry.
- On my team, new ideas are welcomed.[5]

I personally prefer a slightly simpler version of an internal net promoter score (internal NPS), which is adapted from the common NPS measure for customer satisfaction. I used the following four statements in one of my projects, for which each team member had to rate the appropriateness:

- I would recommend the team to my friends as a good place to work.
- I have the tools and resources to do my role well.
- I rarely think about leaving this team or my company.
- My role makes good use of my skills and abilities.

Of course, you can mix or change any of these, but what is important is that you don't look at the absolute value; you need to look at the trend over time. Are you improving the situation in your part of the organization or not? Remember that advice from my old supervisor: you can only control your part of the organization. The corollary to this is, if your part of the organization is not a good place to work, it is all your fault. Being able to measure how culture is changing is important for you, as you otherwise won't know whether things are getting better.

In the activities for this chapter, I added one about measuring how well your managers are managing their teams. I am shocked that almost every time I ask directors what they use to measure the quality of people management in their teams; often, they have no measures whatsoever. Is it any wonder, then, that management is not improving and the culture shift is slow? Don't make the same mistake; make a people measure part of each manager's key performance indicators (KPIs). Use the overall cultural measures discussed here as a shared KPI across all your managers.

In this chapter, I looked at how the role of management shifts when moving away from legacy-style management, and I provided you with some tools to manage knowledge workers. Remember that we are not working in a factory with assembly lines; we are dealing with knowledge workers who perform a creative endeavor. But we are also working with technology, so let's move into the last part of the book, where we discuss the technology aspects of the transformation.

First Steps for Your Organization

Set Up One-On-Ones
It is important to find time in your calendar for each of your directs starting two weeks from now, and be sure to make them recurring meetings on a weekly basis. Make them thirty minutes each, and set the agenda as fifteen minutes for the direct first and fifteen minutes for you second. It is common that the direct may

run over with his/her fifteen minutes, and that's okay. You can find another chance during the week to update the direct with any information that you didn't have time to share during your portion of the one-on-one. I also highly encourage you to take notes and to follow up on the points discussed in the previous week; this will provide a very rich background of information when it comes to performance discussions, providing a progress measure for your direct report.

Define Culture KPIs for Your Managers

You probably have heard the saying "you get what you measure." Though culture is somewhat evasive to metrics, there are some things you can do:

- Leverage the internal NPS that I highlighted in this chapter, and break it down by team as a good high-level measure.
- Measure one-on-ones of your managers. This allows you to measure whether or not your manager builds effective relationships.
- Spot-check the strength of the relationships of your managers. Ask them about some of the fundamental and noninvasive things a boss should know about their people if they have a positive relationship. For example, do they know the names of their directs' kids and partners, and their directs' favorite pastimes?

And yes, you should do the same for yourself to avoid looking for the proverbial speck of sawdust in your manager's eye while ignoring the wooden beam in your own.

Part B Conclusion

This concludes part B of this book, which is about the people and organizational dimension of modern IT delivery organizations. We looked at different ways to provide your employees an organizational structure, the business context, and the necessary feedback to achieve the three motivators that Dan Pink describes: autonomy, mastery, and purpose. We spent additional time diving deep into the organizational and people change that most organizations struggle with during their transformation—the move from testing to quality engineering—which provided an example of how to improve autonomy, mastery, and purpose through organization and process design. Your people will be the factor that makes your transformation succeed or fail, so spend enough time and effort on them during the transformation. In the next part, I will talk about the technical dimension as the last dimension we need to discuss. Technology is at the core of most businesses now, so we need to get this one right too, to be successful.

PART C
Technology and Architecture Aspects

I have been having DevOps discussions for the last few years with many organizations, and usually the discussion revolves around tooling, practices, and culture. This makes sense when you read popular material about DevOps. When we come down to what will influence the results in regard to time to market, however, I think there is a bit of a "dirty secret": architecture is playing a huge role in the final result of your DevOps adoption, yet it is much harder to change and less "sexy" to talk about. The focus on automation and culture is correct, but the third element that far fewer people are talking about is architecture transformation. If you have huge monolithic legacy applications, there will be a limit to what you can achieve. That being said, the tools, methods, and process do play a role as well.

This third part of the book will be the one that is least stable. While I think the first two parts of this book are pretty timeless, this third part might age a bit quicker. I believe that none of the fundamental ideas described in this part are truly new; they just evolved over time and became more relevant and easier to leverage with new technologies and tools. I am looking forward to seeing how things evolve further; trends such as serverless architectures like Amazon Lambda are on the horizon and might require me to rewrite this part in a couple of years. Yet I believe the core of this part of the book will stand the test of time, which is why I decided to include a technology section, taking the risk that my ideas will age.

In part C, I will look at the right way to choose DevOps tooling, what makes a good DevOps architecture, how to evolve your application architecture, how to leverage the relationship between DevOps and cloud computing, what each delivery model looks like, and how these models impact your organization.

CHAPTER 9

Different Delivery Models

Gentlemen, we are going to relentlessly chase perfection,
knowing full well we will not catch it, because nothing is perfect.
But we are going to relentlessly chase it,
because in the process, we will catch excellence.
—**Vince Lombardi**, as quoted in *Game of My Life* by Chuck Carlson

In this chapter, I will describe the three different IT delivery models that are currently being leveraged for successful IT delivery. I will also describe the different capabilities required to make them work. But as I have mentioned a few times already, the challenge goes beyond just the technical uplift to master those capabilities; it depends on the organization to make the appropriate changes across the organization to support the delivery model.

Overview of Delivery Models

I have seen three models that are actively being used or targeted within large organizations to deal with legacy technologies and modern digital technologies at the same time:

1. Continuous delivery: This is the kind of delivery that was described in Jez Humble and David Farley's book on continuous delivery, which allows you to automatically deploy applications

into all the environments from development to production and automatically test them. It is based on persistent environments for deployment.[1]

2. Cloud-enabled delivery: This is the delivery model that Netflix made popular, which creates a new environment each time and destroys the previous one once the new environment has proven to be working. This is effectively a zero-downtime deployment.[2]

3. Container-enabled delivery: This is the delivery model that has become popular with the rise of Docker as a container technology that supports a microservice-based architecture.

There is a fourth delivery model evolving at the moment, based on serverless technologies like Amazon Lambda. At the time I am writing this book, I have not worked with clients to define delivery models for serverless technologies and have not seen a formulated delivery model for them. Perhaps in the next version of this book, I can extend the chapter to include this fourth delivery model.

Within your organization, you will likely have multispeed delivery concerns, which means you will use a mix of these delivery models. When I speak about the transition impacts toward each of these models, remember that this will not be an everyone-at-once approach but will be rather gradual as you move applications and technologies to these delivery models.

Delivery Model A: Continuous Delivery

This model is probably the most well known and has been around for a while, though many companies still struggle to implement it effectively. Continuous delivery means that you can potentially deploy into production with every build, as all the required steps are automated. The word "potentially" is to be read the same way it is used in the Agile community, which means the importance is on the ability to do so, not on actually doing it. You might still choose not to deploy automatically into production—for example, to allow for manual testing or hardening later on. You can leverage this delivery model for both cloud or on-premises environments.

The most common environment pattern into which to deploy is that of persistent environments (e.g., environments that have more than one software drop being deployed). This is often a necessity when working with legacy applications that require a very specific environment setup, so this model is very well suited. The benefits of moving to this model from a more manual, traditional delivery model are a significant improvement of delivery speed, a removal of risk out of your delivery by removing manual steps and increasing the frequency of inspection and feedback, and a reduction of unhelpful noise from the delivery process by increasing transparency across the delivery life cycle.

Description of Capabilities

Continuous delivery is supported by four different capabilities that you need to master. I will only provide a short overview to describe the basics, as there is a lot of material already available to go deeper if you need to.

1. Creating the application: This is one of the core capabilities that enables everything else in the process. This capability covers source-code management; the developer side-quality process (static code analysis, peer reviews, unit testing); the developer work-management process (being able to trace all changes to the functional request associated with it); the compilation, build, and packaging process; and the package management. Mastering this capability is crucial for everything else that comes. While there are successful patterns to leverage here

Model A—Continuous Delivery

Model A deploys applications automatically into persistent environments (either cloud or on premises).

24/7

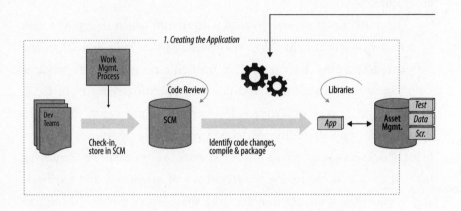

Figure 9.1: Model A—Continuous delivery: Continuous delivery automates delivery to persistent environments

for certain technologies (e.g., you will be able to Google and download Jenkins settings for the building of Java applications), the capability will continue to evolve and will be different in the context of each of the technologies you use.

Ideally, you get to continuous integration (CI), where your application is built with each check-in as a pattern that you can use across all your applications and technology; but often, you will encounter some technologies for which this is just not feasible in an economic fashion. For example, when working with Siebel, our compilation time was over two hours, which is too long for CI. However, automating this capability is probably

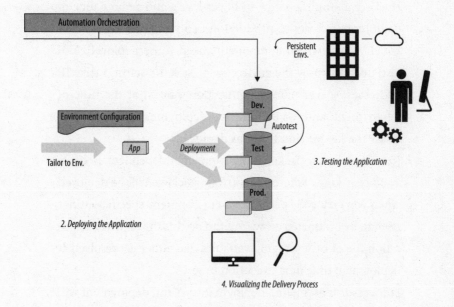

Figure 9.1, cont.

the easiest of them all. The frequency might differ, but there should be very minimal manual effort involved to create a software package from the code in the software configuration management (SCM) system. I have automated this for Siebel, mainframe, and many other technologies. It wasn't always easy but was possible.

2. Deploying the application: Deploying is already a bit more complicated. Overall, it means we are picking up the software package from the package management system and are deploying it into an existing environment. This is also very suitable for full automation. To do that, there are few things to consider.

- Knowing the environment: To deploy successfully, you need to know *where* to deploy the application. It is likely that you have a topology of environments with differences across levels (e.g., multitenancy in lower levels and redundancy of components closer to production), so you need to know on which server which components need to be deployed. You also need to know the environment-specific settings (like IP addresses, server names, connection values) at the time of deployment; and for incremental deployments, you need to know the last version that was deployed.

- Keeping software packages environment independent: Because you never know where the software package will be deployed when you create the package, all environment-specific settings need to be abstracted away. You can do this through a configuration file or by leveraging variables that either get resolved at deployment time or at execution time.

- Full versus incremental deployments: A full deployment will completely replace the application in the environment, which means you don't need to worry about anything. You first delete everything associated with the previous version (after making a backup, of course, in case the new deployment fails) and then deploy the new version into the environment. This full deployment is a lot easier to automate, as it will always follow the same process.

  Incremental deployments are faster but require more complex processes to optimize, which is why organizations often start with full deployments unless the technology does not allow for it (e.g., structure upgrades for transactional tables are always incremental). For incremental deployments, knowing the sequence of incremental packages and which version is in the environment is critical to identigying the right delta set (the files that require changing). It is good practice to automatically validate that the environment is in the expected state before deploying, as the risk of something failing is much higher with incremental deployments. There is also a larger risk of *configuration drift* from manual changes or failed deployments because the environment is not being cleaned up with each deployment.

3. Testing the application: We want to automate as much of the testing process as is feasible and account for the scope of testing, which differs between environments. All the different levels of testing fall into this capability: application test, integration test, performance test, security test, operational readiness test, and anything else that can be automated. Strictly speaking, all the manual testing and how-to-manage manual testing also falls into this capability.

4. Visualizing the delivery process: I believe that you cannot improve what you don't see. The overall delivery model is not something you implement once and that's it; you will have to keep tuning it and improving it. In my experience, the first implementation takes three to six months; then it still changes a lot for the next six to twelve months as you improve. To do this right, you need to have a way of visualizing the end-to-end process and to measure the activities for accuracy and speed. In the past, this was done with text files and Excel sheets like so many things in IT, but new visualization tooling and open-source solutions have allowed this capability to become easy to implement and sexy to use. Capital One went so far as to open-source their internal solution for a DevOps dashboard, which has been adopted by other organizations successfully to manage their DevOps adoption.[3] Out of all the capabilities in this delivery model, this is not the most difficult one but often the most undervalued one. Way too many organizations don't spend enough time and energy on this capability.

Transition Concerns and Organizational Impact

As you transition to continuous delivery, there are a few things you want to consider. First of all, configuration management is crucial; without that, you really can't do anything else. Configuration management allows you to operate at speed. All code (including the tests and the automation code) needs to be in a configuration management system so that it can be accessed and used reliably. The transition to this model requires that your operations and infrastructure teams work closely with the platform team to implement *abstract environment configuration* (a practice that places variables instead of concrete values in configuration files that are replaced at deployment time, when the true values are known). And you will need to have the right environment access for your automation. This will feel like a loss of control to those operations teams, but if you manage this process carefully by involving all groups in the necessary change management, the transition will go much more smoothly.

Change management is also crucial for the transition to this delivery model and all the others. I have been part of several projects to implement new delivery models, and initially, I underestimated the change management efforts (training people, motivating the change in the organization, communicating about the changes and benefits, updating process and role descriptions). After all, if we build a great solution, everyone will jump on the bandwagon, right? Not at all, it turns out. After I noticed this challenge in my first couple of projects, I started to factor this in and staff a dedicated change-management person for my subsequent projects. It turns out that change management is absolutely required and helps everyone on the team. Developers are not that interested in creating training material or process documentation, and the change-management people know how to generate support material that people actually want to use. I think you can come up with a cost-and-effort estimate for this and then double that estimate; and you will probably still look back at the end and think you should have done more.

The organizational changes for the quality organization mentioned in chapter 7 will have to be in place for this model, as you will otherwise have too much friction between the delivery teams who are highly optimized for speed and the separate testing organization.

One last thing to consider is the infrastructure for the tooling platform. Very often, this does not get treated like a production system. But think about it: when your production is down with a defect and your SCM and automation tooling is also down, you are in serious trouble. You should have a production environment of your tooling that you use for your deployments to all environments (from development environment through to production environments), and you will need a development environment of your tooling so that you can continue to test, experiment, and evolve your tooling. You don't want to do this in an environment that you will use for your next production deployment.

Delivery Model B: Cloud-Enabled Delivery

The cloud-based delivery model leverages a couple of practices that became popular after the continuous-delivery concept was already established. The cloud capabilities became more mature; and environment configuration management tools like Chef, Puppet, and Ansible changed the way we think about creating and managing environments. Together, they also account for the main difference from the previous model: we treat environments and infrastructure like code and hence can build additional environments quickly and reliably. Infrastructure as code means that all infrastructure is defined through configuration, which can be stored in a file and, in turn, can be treated as you would treat the source code of a program.

Model B—Cloud-Enabled Delivery

Model B deploys applications automatically after provisioning a new environment from the cloud or data center.

Main difference compared to Model A is the maturing of the infrastructure practices—infrastructure as code.

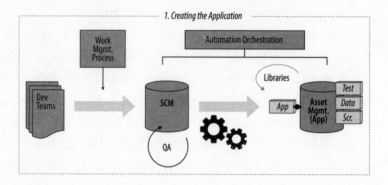

Figure 9.2: Model B—Cloud-enabled delivery: Cloud-enabled delivery creates a new environment with each deployment

In this model, we create a completely new production environment from scratch, including the applications in their latest version. We can then use this environment to test it with a subset of the production traffic to see whether the changes were successful. If we are happy with the result, we can increasingly move more production traffic to the new environment until no traffic goes to the original environment. At this point, we can destroy the old production environment. This is a really low-risk delivery model, as you can manage the risk by the level of testing of the new environment and by the speed of cutover.

Description of Capabilities

Many of the capabilities are very similar but are just being used in the different context of working with brand-new environments each time. This, for example, eliminates the incremental deployment concern mentioned

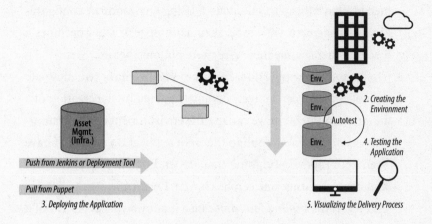

before, as there is nothing to deploy incrementally to. This means you have to find other ways to deal with persistence between environments (e.g., how do you transition all the transactional data or keep it in a different permanent part of the environment?). This gives an indication of the limitation and complexities with this delivery model and why you might not use it for your whole portfolio of applications.

1. Creating the application: This does not change much between the delivery models.
2. Creating the environment: This is the new capability, and it really means having infrastructure as code for everything other than the application code, which we will deploy later. The required infrastructure includes the *compute environments*, the network, the operating system, and the middleware. Because we will need details about the infrastructure for the deployment process, you

want to make sure you gather the configuration information required. This is very similar to what you often do in a more manual fashion in the continuous-delivery model for your persistent environments. Here, the environments change all the time, so you need to have this part automated. Using environment configuration management with tools such as Puppet or Chef becomes a necessity here, while they were more optional before.

3. Deploying the application: In this model, we have two alternate approaches: we can actively deploy triggered by the creation of a new environment, or we can use the environment configuration-management tools to pull in the right application version. I have seen both models and think that, depending on your preference and context, either one can be chosen. Over time, you will likely end up in the *pulling model* because it allows you to get rid of a potentially expensive deployment tool and reduce overall complexity in your setup.

4. Testing the application: This will be pretty much the same as in the continuous-delivery model, but you will probably run more tests related to infrastructure because it gets newly created. And you might run a larger *regression suite*, as you don't have to take production offline while you do it.

5. Visualizing the delivery process: You have a few more aspects to visualize and measure, such as the number of environments currently in use and the speed and reliability of the environment creation with the new environment creation capability, but the overall ideas remain the same.

Transition Concerns and Organizational Impact

Because the infrastructure is not a separate concern from the overall platform anymore, for this delivery model you should merge your infrastructure team with your platform team. It has become more important for that team to understand automation techniques than to be knowledgeable with Windows or UNIX. You still need those skills, but rather than logging into machines, this team focuses on infrastructure as code.

Mastering the capabilities of the continuous-delivery model is really a prerequisite for this model, as any manual steps in this process diminish the benefits you can get out of this. Additionally, the cloud-based model becomes a lot more beneficial if you change the application architecture to leverage the cloud for elasticity and flexibility. I will discuss this further in chapter 12.

Delivery Model C: Container-Enabled Delivery

The fast rise in popularity of Docker (which has made working with Linux containers a lot easier and brought working with containers into the mainstream) has created this new delivery model that many organizations want to leverage. It works extremely well with a microservice architecture due to the low footprint and flexibility of containers. The speed of this delivery model is impressive, as a new container can be created and deployed in seconds. While the previous delivery models required several minutes to several hours, this is, by far, the fastest model. However, this is only true if you have an architecture with relatively small containers. (If you try to run Siebel or SAP in a container, I suspect the experience will be different.) The immutable nature of containers (at least they should be) will force a lot of good behavior in the organization, as it is not possible to patch the containers manually once they have been created.

Description of Capabilities

As with the previous model, the capabilities continue to build on top of each other; and all the capabilities built for the previous model can be

Model C—Container-Enabled Delivery

Model C deploys applications as a set of containers into one or more hosts that are dynamically created.

Main difference compared to Model B is the maturity of the container practices and the more modular application architecture.

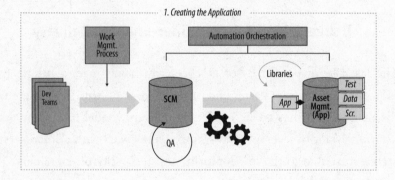

Figure 9.3: Container-enabled delivery manages an application in containers

reused and are, to some degree, prerequisites. The new capabilities have to do with creating and deploying containers.

1. Creating the application: This does not change much between the delivery models.
2. Creating the application container: In addition to the application package that is being stored in the package manager, we are now building application containers that contain everything that is required to run the self-contained application.

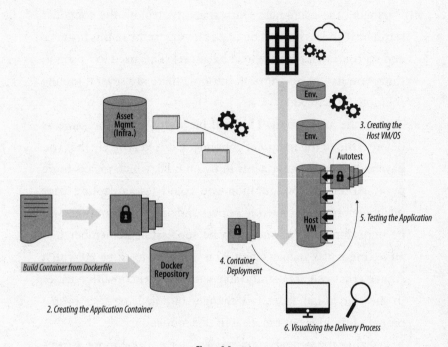

3. Creating the Host VM/OS

Env.

Env.

Asset Mgmt. (Infra.)

Autotest

Host VM

5. Testing the Application

Build Container from Dockerfile

Docker Repository

4. Container Deployment

2. Creating the Application Container

6. Visualizing the Delivery Process

Figure 9.3, cont.

Some aspects of the automated environment provisioning move into this capability, for example, setting up the required data storage, which is within the container rather than in the environment when deploying microservices. Some people do use an environment configuration-management tool for this purpose, but given the immutability of the container, you can use more lightweight approaches for this one-time build. Container management and governance become a new, crucial capability.

3. Creating the host VM/OS: This is very similar to the "creating the environment" capability. You are building a very simple environment that contains the container engine to which the images will be deployed.

4. Deploying the container: This capability deploys the container into a host and switches it on (e.g., moving traffic to this instance and registering it with the load balancer). This used to be something you had to do yourself, but now there are several tooling solutions to help you with it.

5. Testing the application: This will be pretty much the same as before. Due to the nature of containers, it is very likely that you have more small components in this model, which means more permutations of configuration you could test. Adapting your quality approach for a world of ever-moving configurations will be important for this model to be successful. Remember that all testing is risk management. You will have to come up with a strategy that you are comfortable with, as working with releases in the traditional sense (all changes bundled together over a period of time) is not practical in this model.

6. Visualizing the delivery process: You have a few more aspects to visualize and measure, such as the larger number of containers and their health, in addition to the application health with the new container creation and deployment capabilities; but the overall ideas remain the same.

Transition Concerns and Organizational Impact

Because you are now dealing with immutable containers, the governance of the containers becomes a new organizational responsibility. If new vulnerabilities become known, how do you check where you have used certain libraries so that you can update all *container images*? Because you build out containers in layers, you could leverage an old image somewhere in the chain or from a public registry that contains known vulnerabilities. You will have to manage templates that you maintain for the organization to manage the number of flavors. Of course, with containers, you can use lots of different technologies at the same time; but as an organization, you want to manage the number of allowed patterns, as you need to maintain your architecture, and individual teams' preferences for technologies might cause you problems later. Finding the right balance will be something you keep adjusting as you learn more about the usage in your organization.

Similar to the cloud concerns, working with containers means you want to re-architect existing applications to leverage this new paradigm. Just putting your existing application into a large container will not allow you to fully reap the benefits of container-enabled delivery. With this re-architecture activity should also come a reorganizational activity, as it is very inefficient to have an application container owned by more than one team. The best organizational model has the application container fully owned by one team. If the applications are really small, then one team can own multiple applications. If the application container is too large for one team, then it is probably too large in general and should be broken down further. Make Conway's law work for you this time by creating an organizational structure that you would like to have reflected in your architecture.

Evolving Delivery Model: Serverless Delivery

For those of you who have not heard about serverless architectures, this is a service model where you don't run servers as such but rather write a function to perform some business logic for you. When the function is called, an instance is created just for the duration of the *function call*. Amazon Lambda is an example of this architecture. While some of the organizations I work with have experimented with this architecture model, I have

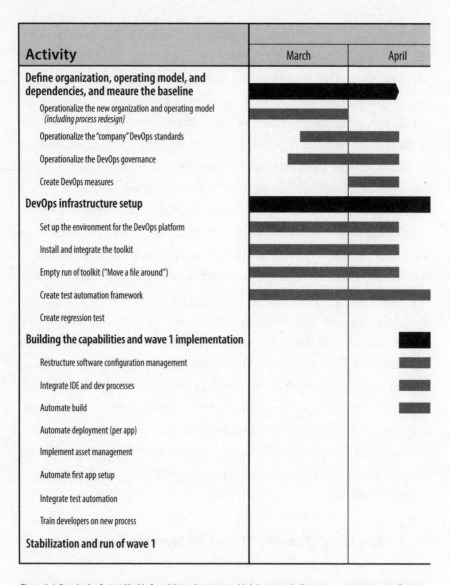

Activity	March	April
Define organization, operating model, and dependencies, and meaure the baseline		
Operationalize the new organization and operating model *(including process redesign)*		
Operationalize the "company" DevOps standards		
Operationalize the DevOps governance		
Create DevOps measures		
DevOps infrastructure setup		
Set up the environment for the DevOps platform		
Install and integrate the toolkit		
Empty run of toolkit ("Move a file around")		
Create test automation framework		
Create regression test		
Building the capabilities and wave 1 implementation		
Restructure software configuration management		
Integrate IDE and dev processes		
Automate build		
Automate deployment (per app)		
Implement asset management		
Automate first app setup		
Integrate test automation		
Train developers on new process		
Stabilization and run of wave 1		

Figure 9.4: Sample plan for initial build of capabilities: Container-enabled changes and infrastructure setup are common first steps

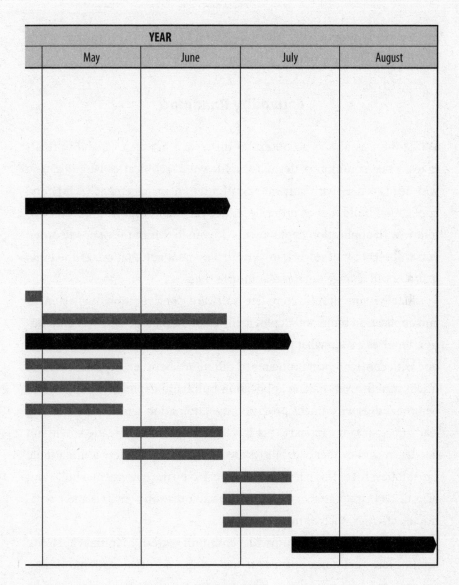

Figure 9.4, cont.

not seen wide adoption yet. You might want to investigate the usage of this and find a use-case model to experiment with in your organization.

Capability Roadmap

While there is always a contextual difference between capability road-maps, I see common patterns to uplift your technical capabilities. You will need to deal with software configuration management (SCM) and application build first in order to reduce the noise, then you will need to follow with application deployments. If you do this in the opposite order, you will see a lot of rework in your deployment automation, as the *build artifacts* will change once you automate them.

Ideally, you should complete software configuration management and application build and deployment automation together. Test automation requires a somewhat predictable environment to work with (e.g., not one with configuration problems or difference between deployments), so it will benefit from having application build and deployment automated beforehand. Environment provisioning automation tends to have a long lead time, so you can start this in parallel so that it is ready when you need it. And the other capabilities are sitting on top of these foundational capabilities. All of this needs to be supported by the incremental build-out of your DevOps platform to support the automation activities and operational activities, such as monitoring.

In Figure 9.4, I have outlined a common pattern of initial capability uplift. Note that some infrastructure setup and organizational design are required before you start jumping into the technical build-out. The build-out follows the software configuration management/build automation first, the deployment automation next, and then followed by the test-automation pattern, which, in my experience, has the highest chance of success.

First Steps for Your Organization

Map Your Application Delivery Models

As I described above, it is not advisable to push all applications into a container-enabled delivery model, as it would not be economical or feasible. In organizations with a large amount of legacy, you will probably have the largest proportion, targeting continuous delivery and cloud-enabled delivery with some container-enabled delivery in your digital applications. And that is realistic. Remember that the goal is to get better; too often, we make perfect the enemy of better. With this in mind, run a workshop where you review your applications and define what your current and ideal delivery model is for each application. You will need to bring people from your infrastructure, your architecture, and your delivery organization into the same room for this. Then do a fit/gap analysis of the capabilities required for the delivery model you assign to each application. Brainstorm a set of initiatives to build the capabilities that are missing. Often, you can reuse capabilities for applications of the same technology stack (e.g., Java) once they are built for another application. Identify those opportunities for reuse. With all these in mind, define a six-month roadmap, and review the roadmap and progress on a monthly basis to reprioritize based on the lessons learned so far.

CHAPTER 10

Application Architecture and Microservices

Architecture depends on its time.
—**Ludwig Mies van der Rohe**,
As quoted in *Programs and Manifestoes on 20th-Century Architecture* by Olrich Conrads

The role of architecture has evolved over the years. When I started doing IT work, the application architecture was something static that described the technology stack and often defined the organizational structure (e.g., a database team, a Java team, and an integration team). Communication between the resulting teams mirrored the data flow in the architecture, with architects mediating conflicts of opinion. Architecture designs had the goal to define the definitive end state, and the resulting diagrams were complex and very detailed, down to the level of modules and function calls. This has changed dramatically over the last few years. Today, architecture is principle based, and the goal of architecture is not to define an end state but to provide flexibility so that it can evolve over time. Ideally, it enables small teams to work independently from each other as functional changes are being made.

I have been spending a lot of time in this book talking about the different capabilities you need in your organization and what organizational changes are required. Yet there is this dirty little secret about the architecture: it is the application architecture that will be one of your main obstacles as you increase your delivery speed. If you think about the typical project, you will probably notice that your speed of delivery is determined by the component that can move the slowest. This is a typical sign of a highly integrated architecture. In such architectures, there is usually some kind of COTS application involved as well, which further slows down delivery due to the monolithic nature of those applications. I am with Jez Humble when he says that culture and architecture are the main obstacles to achieving high performance.[1]

In this chapter, I want to help you drill open your architecture and identify ways to evolve your architecture. The concept of *business IT isomorphism* describes the idea that your architecture should reflect your business, and hence teams can directly support the business without negotiating between parts of the organization. This is obviously very hard to do, and we don't have to go that far, but *monolithic applications* are often not the best model either; we need to find the right balance. This chapter is broken down into three sections: one on architecture principles, one on the evolution of architecture, and one on microservices (no good DevOps book these days can avoid talking about microservices, can it?).

Good Architecture Is Not Easy

Since I started working in IT, architecture has always been one of my main interests. My dad is an architect "in the real sense," as he likes to say (e.g., he builds houses), so perhaps I can at least—in name—continue his legacy as an IT architect. Just like building houses, IT architecture leverages a number of core principles that are required to make the architecture successful and future proof. And trends in architecture evolve—sometimes because of fashion, sometimes because we learned something new.

For the first few years of my career, a few common architecture principles were part of every architect's toolbox:

- KISS—"Keep it simple, stupid" (or more politely, "Keep it short and simple"): A warning to not gold-plate your architecture for situations that will never arise.
- DRY—"Don't repeat yourself": To drive reuse and to avoid the "my wheel is rounder than yours" syndrome.
- Use layers: The typical three-layer architecture that was standard for a long time (presentation layer, business layer, and data layer).
- Encapsulate: Based on object-orientated practices, enforces that a consumer of a service does not need to know how the service is being provided; promotes loose coupling of architectures.

With the advent of cloud computing, the architecture principles have evolved very quickly to adjust to the characteristics of cloud computing. They had to change to derive the maximum value from cloud computing—something many organizations struggle with. Real cloud computing is leveraging the following:

- On demand self-service: We want to be able to automatically create the infrastructure for our service by calling application programming interfaces (APIs) so that no manual intervention is required.
- Resource pooling: The reason cloud computing can be cheaper is because others use what we currently don't use. Dedicated resources are possible on the cloud but limit the cost benefits that would otherwise be possible.
- Network access: We should be able to access our service from anywhere and be able to move the service around to support redundancy and local traffic.
- Rapid elasticity: Scaling up to support more service requests and scaling down to reduce the cost should happen quickly.
- Metered service: We only want to pay for what we use; otherwise, cloud computing can be quite expensive.

Unfortunately, there are a few cloud services out there that don't support all of these capabilities. I worked with a cloud provider once where you had to send in an Excel sheet to get a new machine. This obviously defeats the first characteristic of self-service and impacts the cost profile possible, as there is a long delay between a request to change and the change happening. You are not very elastic when you rely on Excel sheets.

From an architecture perspective, those are the characteristics that we want to leverage to be able to automatically provision our services—to only pay for what we need in regard to infrastructure and to provide a quality service thanks to auto scaling and redundancy.

Here are some of the architecture principles that applications should follow to leverage the cloud:

- Deployed automatically: If you require any manual step in deploying the application, then your hands-off infrastructure provisioning will be limited by the manual deployment steps; you will have just moved the bottleneck.
- Limited resource consumption: To leverage a metered service, we want to shut down components we don't need and always operate at an optimal scale—not too large and not too small.
- Independent of location: Given that certain instances of the application can move around the network, our architecture needs to be able to find each component. This increases the ability to build resiliency to failure.
- Independent to infrastructure and cloud provider: As far as possible, we don't want to be locked into one provider; this allows us more advanced redundancy models and the freedom to look for the best-cost provider. Note that in reality, moving between providers is often not realistic, in which case you want to leverage the rich ecosystem of your chosen provider as much as possible.

- Event driven: Communication should be asynchronous, as the network has to be considered unreliable, allowing the application to deal better with network latency. Synchronous calls consume resources in wait stage and can have significant performance impacts.
- Resilient to latency: Given that we cannot guarantee the network response, our applications need to deal with this and work around the user impact of the latency.
- Horizontally scalable: We want to scale by provisioning additional nodes, which means our process should be parallelizable. This allows us to route requests to any instance, which increases the resilience of the architecture in turn.
- And, of course, secure: Security across all levels of the architecture continues to be a concern of your architects; it cannot be delegated to the cloud provider.*

Evolving Your Architecture Over Time

Most organizations currently use an architecture model based on a strong core set of systems that rely on commercial-off-the-shelf (COTS) products, mainframe technologies, or something similar. On top of this core set of systems sits an *access layer*. This access layer is highly dependent on the core systems to provide any meaningful business service. Realistically, before an organization with this architecture model in place can make any significant change, they will need to update the whole monolithic application. This is the architecture status quo in many organizations.

---

* Another good set of architecture principles are those of twelve-factor applications, which you can find detailed by Adam Wiggins at 12Factor.net.

Strategy 1: Decoupling

One strategy we used with a public-service client that had a large mainframe setup was to decouple the architecture by creating an *abstraction layer* between the core system and the access layer. In our example, we had the mainframe team create *consumable services* our *front-end team* could leverage. Both teams were working in an Agile fashion, and we used the common planning event (similar to the PI planning from SAFe) to align on which services were made available at what point. The front-end team could evolve independently as long as they consumed the service provided by the mainframe application. When they required a new service, this was prioritized in the mainframe team's backlog. Practically, this was a *two-speed delivery model* enabled by a service layer as a clutch between the two different speeds.

Strategy 2: Going on a Diet

In this strategy, you are basically addressing the need for flexibility and speed by paying down your technical debt and making the core more agile. This is considered a very conservative strategy; but in certain contexts, especially where heavy customizations have made COTS products difficult to maintain, this can provide some breathing room before you decide to take a further step with a different strategy for your re-architecting effort.

With one of our clients, we looked at the state of the Siebel application we used and how it evolved over time. It became clear to us that we had accrued a large amount of technical debt over time. For example, some customizations we made had, in the meantime, become integrated into the core product in a more efficient way. We had also customized the product to a degree that made the application difficult to maintain— just so that some special cases could be covered by the same system. We decided to remove customizations and to let the application go on a diet. Over time, this allowed us to reduce the delivery cycle time, reduce the cost of change, and make the code a lot more maintainable.

Strategy 3: Let's Try It on the Side

This strategy is one that I have seen becoming more popular in the last few years. Rather than working with the core, an alternative architecture is created for a certain part of the business. This new architecture is built in a nearly *green field setting* (starting from scratch without legacy applications) with limited integration to the old core or the old access layer. In this new system, modern architecture principles and technical practices are used. Often, a separate organizational structure is created to support this new system (e.g., a digital team).

One of my clients created a digital team that worked very differently from the old technology teams supporting the core. The real challenge is that at some point, you need to either integrate the two parts of the business and make sure that the good practices from the new organization and architecture are adopted by the core as well, or you need to gradually push more and more functionality into the new organization following the strangler pattern until the old systems and organizations can be "shut down." With our client, we went down the integration path and used the proven ways of working from the new architecture to uplift the existing legacy applications and support a faster way of delivery.

Strategy 4: Erode the Core with Microservices

This last strategy is the most popular these days. With it, we erode the core by creating microservices that support parts of the business so that less and less functionality is used from the core systems. We use the strangler pattern again to slowly move toward a microservice architecture.

I will spend the next section of this chapter on microservices to give you a better idea of how to use them.

Introduction to Microservices

As I mentioned, microservices have become extremely popular, yet the term is often used in a vague fashion, as there is no really good and clear definition that tells you when you have a microservice. Overall, you can consider microservices the other extreme of a monolithic application.

Let's talk a little bit about monoliths, because there are good reasons for using monoliths in certain circumstances. If you have a relatively simple application, using microservices might be overkill. A monolithic application is often easier to debug and test because it has fewer moving parts, which might cause you problems. And let's face it, monoliths are a lot easier to explain and manage—an evolving microservice architecture with hundreds of microservices that are being developed and deployed independently will cause many organizations to have issues with their governance approach. If something doesn't need to evolve, then you probably can't justify breaking it up into microservices either. The cost of designing a predictable microservice architecture is higher than a monolithic application due to the introduction of additional variables, such as network latency, backward version compatibility, and message sequencing.

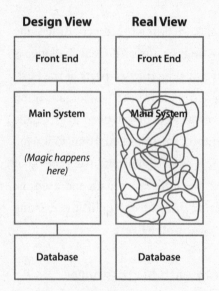

Figure 10.1:
Design view versus real view:
Simple diagrams do not equal simple architectures

On the flip side, while monolithic applications look nice and neat from the outside, and they behave very well in architecture diagrams, they tend to be placeholders for "magic happens here." This means the complexity is absorbed into that "black box." I have seen enough Siebel and some SAP code that tells me that this perceived simplicity is just hidden complexity. And of course, all of this becomes worse the larger the monolith becomes and the larger the number of people who have been involved with its creation over time.

Microservices make the complexity more visible. As far as catchy quotes go, I like Randy Shoup's from YOW15: "Microservices are nothing more than SOA done properly."[2] Within this lies most of the definition of a good microservice: It is a service (application) that serves one purpose; it is self-contained and independent; it has a clearly defined interface and isolated persistence (even to the point of having a database per service).

Here's a helpful analogy, which I heard for the first time in a talk by James Lewis:

> This, milord, is my family's axe. We have owned it for almost nine hundred years, see. Of course, sometimes it needed a new blade. And sometimes, it has required a new handle, new designs on the metalwork, a little refreshing of the ornamentation. . . . But is this not the nine-hundred-year-old axe of my family? And because it has changed gently over time, it is still a pretty good axe, y'know. Pretty good.[3]

This evolution of the pieces that make the axe still good after nine hundred years is what you want your architecture to be like. Rather than having transformational IT projects every few years that are risky and cause a lot of disruption, you want a constant evolution of pieces so that the architecture renews itself.

What Are the Benefits of Microservices?

Over time, everyone in IT has learned that there is no end-state architecture. The architecture of your systems always evolves, and as soon as one implementation finishes, people are already thinking about the next change. In the past, updating the architecture to a newer version has been quite difficult to achieve, as you had to replace large systems. With microservices, you create an architecture ecosystem that allows you to change small components all the time and avoid big-bang migrations. This flexibility means you are much faster in evolving your architecture. Additionally, the structure of microservices means that teams have a greater level of control over their service, and this ownership will likely see your teams become more productive and responsible as they develop their services. The deployment architecture and release mechanism becomes significantly easier; you don't have to worry about dependencies that need to be reflected in the release and deployment of services. This, of course, comes with increased complexity in testing, as you have many possible permutations of services to deal with. Automation and intelligent testing strategies are very important.

When Should You Use Microservices?

Microservices are relevant in areas that you know your company will invest in over time. Areas where speed to market is especially important are a good starting point, as speed is one of the key benefits of microservices. Dependency-ridden architecture gets bogged down for many reasons, from developers having to learn about all the dependencies of their code to the increasing risk of components being delayed in the release cycle. Microservices won't have those issues due to their independence, which is built into the architecture. Of course, this is only true if you follow good architecture principles for your microservices; no one prevents you from building small integrated services, but we wouldn't call them microservices.

Another area to look for is applications that cannot continue to scale vertically in an economic fashion. The *horizontal scaling* abilities of the microservices specific to those services increase the possibilities of finding economic scaling models. And of course, a move toward microservices requires investment, so go for an area that can afford the investment and where the challenges mentioned earlier are providing the burning platform to start your journey.

What Does It Take to Be Successful with Microservices?

This will not surprise you, but I'll say it anyway: the level of extra complexity that comes with independently deployable services might also exist in production in multiple versions, which means you really need to know your stuff. And by this, I mean you need to be mature in your engineering practices and have a well-oiled deployment pipeline with "automated everything" (continuous integration, deployment, testing). Otherwise, the effort and complexity in trying to maintain this manually will quickly outweigh the benefits of microservices. I was working with a client who had a small number of microservices (fewer than ten) but did not have the maturity required to scale any further, because they still had to manually build and test those microservices. For them, the benefits of microservices were still out of reach until they could fix the engineering maturity.

Conway's law says that systems resemble the organizational structure they were built in.[4] Therefore, to build microservices, we need to have mastered the Agile and DevOps principle of cross-functional teams (and ideally, align them to your value streams). These teams have full ownership of the microservices they create (from cradle to grave). This makes sense if the services are small and self-contained, as having multiple teams involved (DBAs, .NET developers, etc.) would just add overhead to small services. As you can see, my view is that microservices are the next step of maturity from DevOps and Agile, because they require organizations to have already mastered both (or at least be close).

How Can You Get Started with Microservices?

If your organization is ready (which, as with Agile and DevOps, is a prerequisite for the adoption of microservices), go ahead and choose a pilot and create a microservice that adheres to the definition (service for one purpose; self-contained; independent, with clearly defined interface and isolated persistence) and is of real business value (e.g., something that is being used a lot, is customer facing, and is in a suitable technology stack). Your first pilot is not likely to be a runaway success, but you will learn from the experience. Microservices will require investment from the organization, and the initial value might not be clear cut (as just adding the functionality to the monolith might be cheaper at first); but in the long term, the flexibility, speed, and resilience of your microservice architecture will change your IT landscape. Will you end with a pure microservice architecture? Probably not. But your core services might just migrate to an architecture that is built and designed to evolve, and hence serve you better in the ever-changing marketplace.

First Steps for Your Organization

Identify Your Architecture Evolution Strategy
Invite your architects to a workshop about architecture strategies. Let them explain what the current plan is, and try to map this back to the architecture evolution strategies I have highlighted in this chapter: decoupling your architecture; removing technical debt; creating a new architecture on the side or eroding the old

architecture core. Then discuss alternative approaches with them and see whether you can come to an aligned strategy that will provide more decoupled services over time. Make sure that with this architecture evolution strategy, related capabilities are covered too. Refer back to the delivery models and their associated capabilities to make sure your architects are not talking just about the system blueprints but also about the capability build-out to support the architecture with the right engineering practices.

CHAPTER 11

Running Applications and Your DevOps Tools Efficiently

> Not everything that counts can be counted,
> and not everything that can be counted counts.
> —**William Bruce Cameron**, *Informal Sociology: A Casual Introduction*
> *to Sociological Thinking*

I have spoken about the delivery models in an earlier chapter, and in my experience, people spend a lot of time with the development aspects. The focus was more on the "Dev" aspect of DevOps. In this chapter, I will speak about the operational aspects. Three different topics I will cover here: what modern operations looks like for applications (including monitoring and application maintenance), what it means to run the DevOps platform, and how the uplift of the DevOps capabilities has allowed for smaller and smaller batch sizes to be economical and hence reduce the risk for operations.

Modern Application Operations

Traditionally, organizations considered application support in production to be a necessary evil and dealt with it with the legacy mind-set of finding a provider who could provide this at low cost. After all, you just have to keep it running, and any changes should be minimal. This is, unfortunately, a bad approach to running applications, as applications deteriorate over time. You will need an increasing amount of effort to maintain them and will accrue further technical debt. I have heard others refer to a 50% rule, which I like: If you spend more than 50% of the operations teams' effort on firefighting, you've lost the fight. You will now spend more and more time firefighting, as you don't spend enough time on improving your automation and improving the code base of your application for maintainability.

I think with web-based services, the balance has shifted a little bit, and a lot of the maintenance of websites has become business critical. As a result, operations has been brought in-house over time, yet in many legacy organizations, the investment continues to be on new capabilities and not on improving operations.

Running applications in production used to be a very reactive activity: when there was a problem, someone got paged and solved the problem. In between those calls, you would work on a list of known problems to resolve or you would make up for the overtime incurred when solving issues by taking time off work. A new culture is evolving in modern organizations where this is different, and issues in production are not seen as problems but rather as a chance to improve production further. Let me illustrate this with an example.

I was sitting in a coffee shop in Portland, Oregon, with one of my friends in the DevOps community, and we ordered coffee. While we did so, he got a text message that there was a problem in production. I expected him to get up and jump on a conference call as is the custom in so many organizations. Instead, when I asked him about it, he indicated that we should finish our coffee first. Before we had finished our coffee, he got another message saying that everything was all right again. I was impressed and told him that he must have a pretty good team on board to fix problems so quickly. His answer surprised me. He said that his team is pretty slow at solving problems. He went on to explain that his team is deliberately slow at resolving issues when they occur, because they don't want to waste the opportunity to find out what went wrong. They use the information to identify which automatic problem identification could be done and then which automatic treatment could resolve it; only then do they fix the problem. In this instance, the problem was something that the system was autocorrecting. He then explained to me that organizations have two choices—the virtuous cycle, where more and more time can be used to improve the production system proactively, and the vicious cycle, where you just keep fixing the problems that occur without improving the overall system. I know where I stand and have been using his approach for my projects since.

In an advanced-maturity state, the production system should operate on the basis that very limited manual intervention is required.

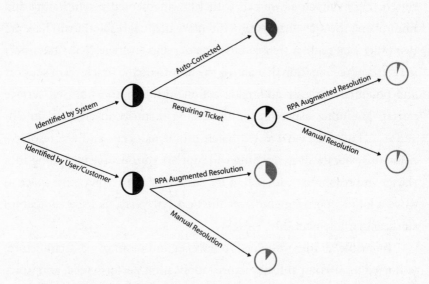

Figure 11.1: Advanced maturity state: Modern operations works based on the principle to minimize work that needs to be done

Consider Figure 11.1: Through the right monitoring, we want to have the ability to find about half the problems ourselves, as problems identified by the system, without the user having to notify us (problems identified by the user). Most of those should not even require a problem ticket to be created but rather are addressed by action recipes that the team has created over time, and those problems are automatically resolved (auto-corrected). For the others that we don't have automated recipes for yet, we require a ticket, which we can automatically create. Many tend to fall in common categories so that we can support the resolution with things like *robotic process automation* (*RPA*-augmented resolution) to minimize rework and manual effort (a lot of the effort tends to go into a small set of common tasks that can be supported with RPA).

But there will be a small number of problems that are completely new or for which there is no automatic solution; those will get assigned to the operations team for action and manual resolution. For the problems that are being identified by users, we will use the same logic—for example, supporting as much as we can with RPA-augmented resolutioning and minimizing the ones that require intensive manual resolutions. There are two other aspects that we need to consider and leverage: The first aspect is a self-service function that allows the user to do the first level of support and potentially trigger automatic actions directly from the self-service portal. The other aspect is the increasing maturity in artificial intelligence. A lot of data is created when problems occur and are resolved; using this data for deep learning will support your people in finding root causes and resolutions. It's still in its early days, but I expect this space to drive a lot of improvements over the next few years, as I see companies starting to implement this.

To enable all this, you need to have a good monitoring architecture: you need to monitor infrastructure, application performance, and functionality. But with a lot of monitoring comes a lot of responsibility. It is very easy to drown people with all this information. Extensive monitoring is good, as it provides data; and data is the basis for analysis and future automation. Extensive notifications become a problem, though. So, manage your notifications based on impact—don't page an operational person in the middle of the night if the server outage will not actually impact the user experience or if automated recipes are available for the problem.*

Defining and Running the DevOps Platform

Running the DevOps platform should also be considered an operational activity that is treated with the same seriousness. I like the way the Open Group has termed one of their reference models "IT4IT,"[1] as this falls into that category. You are running an IT system to support business IT systems. Keeping this fully operational should have a similar priority to your business production systems and should not be something that is driven from a developer machine or sandbox environment. Consider the situation where you have an incident in production and require a fix. If at the same time your source control is not available or corrupt, you are in trouble. Your DevOps platform needs to be designed with operational requirements in mind.

Similar to the earlier discussion on how to choose business applications, we have a problem for DevOps tools.† What are the right DevOps tools? I will not go into specific tools; instead, I will tell you what I am looking for in DevOps tools beyond the functionality they provide. In my experience, you can build good *DevOps tool chains* with just about any tool, but some tools might take more effort to integrate than others.

Obviously, DevOps tools should support DevOps practices and promote the right culture. This means the tools should work beyond their

---

* *Site Reliability Engineering: How Google Runs Production Systems* by Betsy Beyer, Chris Jones, Jennifer Petoff, and Niall Richard Murphy talks about good monitoring practices that can help you make the right choices.

† It seems that new DevOps tools appear on the market every month. This is extenuated by the fact that it is difficult to classify all the tools in the DevOps toolbox. One of the best reference guides is the XebiaLabs periodic table of DevOps, which is well worth checking out.

own ecosystem. It is very unlikely that a company only uses tools from one vendor or ecosystem. Hence, the most important quality of a tool is the ability to integrate it with other tools (and yes, possibly be able to replace it at a later stage, which is important in such a fast-moving market). As a result, the first check for any DevOps tool involves judging how well APIs are supported. Can you trigger all functionality that is available through the UI via an API (command-line or programming-language based)?

We should treat our tools just like any other application in the organization, which means we want to version-control them. The second check is determining whether all configurations of the tool can be version-controlled in an externalized configuration file (not just in the application itself). Related to the second point is the functionality to be able to support multiple environments for the tool (e.g., development versus production). How easy is it to promote configuration across those environments? How can you merge configuration of different environments (code lines)? We want everyone in the company to be able to use the same tool. This has implications for the license model that is most appropriate. Of course, open source works for us in this case, but what about commercial tools? They are not necessarily bad. What is important is that they don't discourage usage. For example, tools that require agents should not price for every agent, as this means people will be tempted to not use them everywhere. Negotiate an enterprise-wide license or "buckets of agents" so that each usage does not require a business case.

Visualization and analytics are important aspects of every DevOps tool chain. To make them work, we need easy access to the underlying data; that means we likely want to export data or query data. If your data is stored in an obscure data model or if you have no way to access the underlying data and export it for analysis and visualization, then you will require additional overhead to get good data. Dashboards and reports within the tool are no replacement, as you likely want to aggregate and analyze across tools.

I think these criteria are all relatively obvious, and what is surprising is how few tools adhere to these. Open-source tools are often better at this but might require a higher level of technical skills in your team to set up and maintain. I hope tool vendors will start to realize that if they want to provide DevOps tools, they need to adhere to the cultural values of DevOps to be accepted in the community; otherwise, they will continue to lose to open-source tooling. In the meantime, think about what matters most for you and your organization and then compromise on criteria where you have to. There is not one right tooling architecture.

But how do you manage this ever-evolving space of DevOps tools? I think you need to take a practical approach, as you will need some standardization but want to remain flexible as well. In general, in a large organization, it makes sense to have a minimal set of tools to support for several reasons:

- optimizing license cost
- leveraging skills across the organization
- minimizing complexity of integration between tools

Yet on the other side, some tools are much better for specific contexts than others (e.g., your .NET tooling might be different from your mainframe tooling). And there are new tools coming out all the time.

To remain somewhat flexible, I have implemented the following approach:

- Start with a small set of standard tools in your organization.
- Allow a certain percentage of teams to diverge from the standard for a period of time (three to six months, perhaps).
- At the end of the "trial period," gather the evidence and decide what to do with the tool in discussion.
  - Replace the current standard tool.

– Get it added as an additional tool for specific contexts.

– Discard the tool, and then transition the team back to the standard tool.

Everything we said about keeping production systems running applies to our DevOps platform as well. I have highlighted in the delivery models section of this book that from the beginning, you need to set up an environment topology that allows you to evolve your DevOps platform with production and development environments. As you can see, the term "IT4IT" from the Open Group is pretty accurate.

Managing Smaller Batches of Changes

One of the most important drivers for effort and risk in production changes is the batch size. In the past, the batch size has been quite large, as many changes were bundled together into annual or quarterly releases. This was done not only because people believed that it was less risky to deal with fewer larger changes but also for the economic reasons of reducing the cost of such events. The optimal batch size is determined by both the transaction cost for deploying a batch and the opportunity cost of holding the finished functionality back until the next release (see Figure 11.2). Because the cost of deploying was high in the past (including quality control, fixing problems in production post-deployment, etc.), batch sizes had to be larger, but everything that is discussed in part C of this book reduces the transaction cost and hence allows us to reduce the batch size (see Figure 11.2). This, in turn, increases your speed of delivery, reduces the complexity of each change, and reduces the total cost of deploying and running the change in production. So, besides the business benefits of small batch sizes that we discussed earlier, there are practical operational benefits to small batch sizes too.

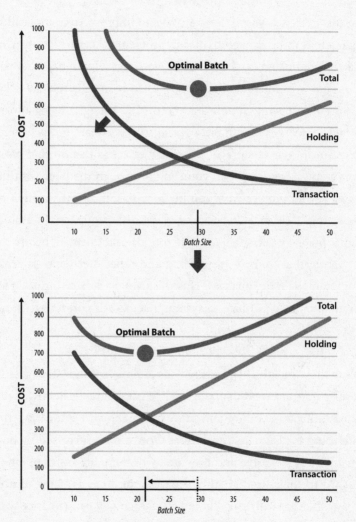

Figure 11.2: Reducing transaction costs enables smaller batch sizes

First Steps for Your Organization

Run Problem-Ticket Analysis

In this exercise, we will look at ways to improve your application operations through analysis of your problem tickets to identify what can be automated. As I said before, you have a lot of data that you don't use to its full potential. Get your hands on this problem-ticket data, and run some simple analysis over it. I suggest using a word cloud to identify common wording (e.g., "restart server," "reset password," "out of storage"); then try to categorize on that basis. Once you have done that, you can go through the ones with the highest count to see what can be done to improve the system by resolving it either automatically or with the support of automation. It usually takes two to three rounds of refinement before the categorization—based on wording and other metadata—is accurate enough for this analysis. This will give you the starting point for your automated production system that can self-correct over time.

Review Your DevOps Tools

With the principles of good DevOps tooling in mind (strong APIs, configuration as code, supportive licensing model), sit down with the architects in your organization and make a list of the tools you are using for DevOps capabilities. You will be surprised by how many tools you have and how many of them are overlapping in regard to their functionality. Analyze the tools for how future-ready they are (utilizing Table 11.1, which you can enhance with further criteria specific to your context), and define your weak spots, where you have tools that are really not compatible with the DevOps way of working and are holding you back. Identify a strategy to replace these tools in the near future.

Criteria	Tool A	Tool B
API support		
Configuration management		
Multienvironment / code-branch support		
License model		
Data access		

Table 11.1: DevOps tools review: DevOps tools should follow DevOps good practices themselves

CHAPTER 12

The Cloud

Jay: It went up! It went up to the cloud!
Annie: And you can't get it down from the cloud?
Jay: Nobody understands the cloud! It's a f***ing mystery!
—*Sex Tape* (movie)

U nfortunately for many organizations, the cloud is still somewhat mysterious—not the concept of the cloud but why they are not seeing the benefits that were promised to them. In this chapter, I want to help demystify this aspect and discuss some of the challenges I see with cloud migration and what it takes for your organization to really benefit from leveraging the cloud. The focus in this chapter is on adopting cloud-based infrastructure and managing it. We already discussed the considerations for software as a service in chapter 3 and application architecture in chapter 10. Together, these give you good coverage of the different aspects of leveraging cloud-based services.

While we will discuss cost benefits primarily in this chapter, one should not forget the other benefits and risks of the cloud. Examples of additional benefits: the ease of setting up redundancy for resilience, the scalability of resources, and the strong ecosystem of related services that you would otherwise have to build yourself. On the risk side: the dependency on a third-party provider, the challenges with data sovereignty, and the risk of being attacked because you are on a popular platform.

Basic Principles of Cloud Economics

Before I discuss some of the considerations for cloud migration, it is probably helpful for us to level set on the economic model of the cloud. If you look at a straight comparison of cloud services and on-premises solutions, then at the very basic level, the cloud solution is going to be more expensive (e.g., having one fully utilized server on premises is cheaper than having one fully utilized service in the cloud). Some people have done modeling for this, and you can find a few models on the internet. It is inherently difficult to do the comparison, though, as the supporting costs from the ecosystem are hard to calculate. From my experience with my clients, I can tell you that migrating applications straight to the cloud often does not provide the expected significant savings unless you invest in some refactoring or re-architecting.

The economics of the cloud are based on the sharing of resources, so that everyone only pays for what they consume, and any excess capacity can be used by others. On the flip side, this means that services with high variability will benefit more from the cloud model. The benefit of this depends on how quickly the service can respond to a change in demand (see Figure 12.1).

It is important to understand this basic model of fluid capacity that responds to the need of the application when considering an adoption of the cloud and the impact your architecture will have on the benefits of the cloud.

Cloud Architecture Considerations

If you think through the considerations above, you realize that a monolithic application provides a lot less opportunity to respond with the same level of variability. If any part of the application is running out of capacity, the whole application needs to be replicated; hence a new instance needs

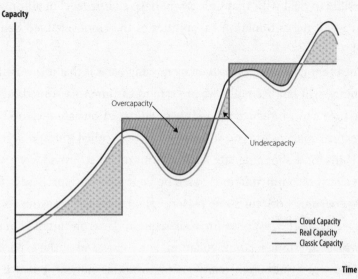

Figure 12.1: Capacity versus time: When done correctly, cloud capacity moves according to the need

to be created. Imagine you have several business channels, and only one of them is popular on the weekend (e.g., your internet channel). In that case, you only want to scale this business channel while the other ones run at minimum capacity during that same time. If everything is in one monolith, you will have to run your whole business at the same capacity and pay a lot more.

But if the architecture allows for separate services to be scaled independently (similar to how we described this for microservices in the architecture chapter), then the scaling becomes a lot more granular and therefore useful to optimize for cost. This is the major benefit of the cloud.

However, the more you break down the architecture to benefit from the above consideration, the more moving pieces you have to deal with. With more moving pieces, your ability to manage multiple versions needs to improve. Rather than managing twenty applications, you might have to manage 150 services, each with their own *versioning*. It is nearly impossible to deal with that unless you have a large level of automation in place—all the automation capabilities of the cloud-enabled delivery model.

The other challenge with so many moving parts is that it is very likely that things will fail. Actually, we are safe to assume that something will fail, so how can we reduce the points of failure in our architecture? The architecture concept for you to consider here is called *graceful degradation*. Think of a shopping site such as Amazon that provides you with personalized recommendations based on your previous purchases. If that service does not work for some reason, rather than not showing you the site or delaying the response for your request, Amazon might choose to show you some static recommendation. For you as a user, the experience is slightly worse (although many people wouldn't notice), but it is still much better than getting a page error or time-out. Leveraging this idea of graceful degradation works in many contexts but not *all*, and it will usually be a cheaper alternative to keeping the whole end-to-end availability at very high availability.

Cloud-based architecture often involves using packages or templates (like Docker templates) from cloud repositories, which is great from a reuse perspective. But doing this does not mean you don't have to manage those dependencies. For example, a very small package nearly caused major internet outages in 2016 when a developer named Azer Koçulu took a package off the internet that was reused in many other systems and subsequently broke those systems unintentionally.[1] Another risk is that those templates you use contain vulnerabilities that you are not aware of. Josh Corman spoke about this at the 2015 DevOps Enterprise Summit using some research he had done to see how many open-source or third-party components are in Docker templates (many are unknown, similar to the example of the small package earlier). He found that over 20% of Docker templates had known vulnerabilities. This exposes you to a lot of risks.[2] So, both unavailability (or version change) as well as known vulnerabilities (that are hidden in your templates) are things you need to actively manage for your application.

One of my clients decided on a very conservative strategy to create an internal repository of every component they leverage. With that in mind, they download and store a copy from the public cloud for every version they use and actively manage these versions. For them, new versions are not automatically used, and they need to spend the effort to monitor for new versions and then choose to pull them in. But it means they can prevent unavailability and version conflict, and they have the direct ability to scan for known vulnerabilities. This might not be a strategy for everyone due to the cost, but you can dial the risk up and down by choosing how actively you manage this part of your cloud architecture.

Cloud Governance

All the flexibility that the cloud provides is fantastic. The typical bottleneck of projects (due to a lack of environments) all but disappears, and delivery capacity is freed up. But with all this flexibility come a few new problems. In the past, adding more cost to your infrastructure bill required detailed planning, and there was a high level of scrutiny. But now with the cloud, any developer with a company credit card can buy cloud services. One client I worked with opened public cloud infrastructure to their developers, and in the first month, the environment budget for the first half year was consumed. As you can imagine, that was a lesson for the organization.

At the same time, if instead of the lengthy procurement process of infrastructure you now have a lengthy approval process for cloud infrastructure, then you have not gained a lot with your transition. The trick is to find the right balance. You will have to find a new governance model that considers both cost and speed so that teams can make the right decision when provisioning environments.

Logical environment management remains a function required when you work with the cloud. In an on-premises model, the environment-management function manages who can use an environment at which point, and which configuration is being used in that environment at each point in time. With the cloud, you also want to make sure that certain standards of your organization are being followed and that templates are being provided for this. Additionally, you want to make sure that you have a strategy for how the individual environments are being used and where the applications are coming together to be tested against each other. After all, you want to make sure that the configuration of the applications that will be in production together gets tested somewhere. The proliferation of environments and associated application configurations can make that a real challenge unless someone keeps control over that.

Organizations can get around some of these aspects by leveraging a cloud-management system or broker system that allows you to reflect your organizational context within the management console. Such a system also makes sure that security standards are being followed, that only approved templates are being provisioned, and that budget constraints are considered. Ideally, such a system would also be able to identify the cheapest public cloud provider and provision the environment with that provider; but as of writing this book, the reality is that the ability to move between providers is a lot less realistic than one would hope. Each cloud provider offers idiosyncratic services that supply additional benefits but also create a level of lock-in. The management functions of such a broker system, however, are a significant benefit. Cloud is beneficial when you have more moving parts; with more moving parts comes the need for better governance. Ask yourself how good your environments' management is at the moment and how many environments you have. Now consider yourself with a cloud architecture in which you have ten or a hundred times more environments. Would your current environment-management approach still work?

Site Reliability Engineering

When working with the cloud, the traditional operations idea also needs to be overhauled. The term that is most commonly associated with this change is *site reliability engineering* (SRE), which Google made popular.

Given that a cloud-based architecture works on many smaller components, which all operate with redundancy, it is very unlikely that you will suffer a complete outage (although you will if your cloud provider has a full outage). What this means in return is that instead of the traditional availability-measure time period:

$$\frac{unavailable\ time\ of\ component}{time\ period}$$

(which made sense when you monitored a small number of components), you should move toward service availability (e.g., can a certain service be provided with the specific performance and quality):

$$\frac{number\ of\ total\ requests - failed\ requests}{number\ of\ total\ requests}.$$

To manage the results of this availability measure, the *concept of error budgets* is commonly used. The idea is that each service has a certain budget of times when the service does not work, either because of a planned activity (such as an upgrade or deployment) or due to a problem. With this budget set, the teams can, to some degree, choose how to use it (e.g., if they are sure a deployment will only consume 5% of that budget but it goes wrong and consumes 25%, then there will be less budget for other activities). This incentivizes the teams to find lower-impact solutions to upgrades and deployments and better ways to keep the service available over time. It is also frequently used in DevOps circles to align the incentives of the Dev and Ops teams by having this common budget of unavailability across both functions. Cloud-based solutions are often developed by both teams to minimize the impact on the budget.

A related measure that helps you to consume less error budget and is often called *the* key metric for DevOps is *mean time to recovery* (MTTR). This is the time it takes for service to become available again after a failure has been detected. Combined with *mean time to discovery* (MTTD), which is the time it takes from the time the service fails to the time the problem has been identified, these two metrics drive your unplanned unavailability. In your DevOps or SRE scorecard, you want these two metrics—together with the availability metric—to be really visible for everyone so that you can measure improvements over time.

Monitoring in an SRE model (and really, not only then) should fall into three categories:

1. Alerts: This is when you need to actively do something to restore the service. Remember that we are not just after uptime here; so if a server or service fails but has no immediate user impact, then we don't want to call an engineer in the middle of the night. We want to keep that escalation for when we really need it. Otherwise, our on-call engineers will burn out easily.
2. Tickets: These are problems we find and need to do something about but not immediately. The monitoring system should create a ticket, which then gets prioritized in the SRE backlog and actioned during normal business hours.
3. Logs: This will come in handy when we have a problem, but it will also be useful for proactive analysis of trends and identification of areas that need improvement.

Site reliability engineering has formalized the usage of the scientific method as part of the continuous improvement activities. So, for every improvement, you should predict what kind of impact it will have, measure the baseline, and after the implementation, check whether the improvement has really helped. As I mentioned earlier in the transformation governance chapter, this rigor is important to drive improvements.

It is, however, important that the pursuit of improvements includes your team and is not some kind of punishment for not having done it before. The term *blameless postmortem* has been coined to symbolize the shift from root-cause analysis, where the organization tries to find out which team or person caused the problem, to a forward-looking culture in which a problem is used to identify a way to improve the system and make it harder for people to make the same mistake again. As I mentioned in chapter 8, Etsy is on record for having each of their new IT employees deploy into production. You might think this is risky, but Etsy argues that if a newbie can break production, they clearly have not built a system strong enough to find the simple problems that a newbie could cause. This focus on improving the system to make it better for people to use is similarly ingrained in the DevOps and SRE communities.

What helps with this culture shift is that the DevOps practices of DevOps and cloud make change management a lot less risky. After all, deployments into production can be seen as just another testing phase. If you only deploy to a small subset of production and test the new version with a small data flow from production—we call this *canary testing*, after the canaries used in coal mines to identify gas leaks—then any negative impact is contained by the amount of data we have pushed to the new version. We can regulate the speed of rollout against our appetite for risk and rollback changes if we really need to.

Additionally, the same technical setup that allows canary testing also enables us to do A/B testing, which means we can run two different configurations of a service in production and see which one produces better results; then we roll that one out to the full production environments once we are convinced that we have found the better alternative.

I want to mention two more things that differentiate a good cloud architecture and the organizations that run them. Firstly, the forecasting abilities: cloud providers will allow you to dynamically scale which will work for a certain range of your services. Different circumstances might still require you to do your own forecasting (and you should always be doing some forecasting yourself). In Australia, we have a horse race called the Melbourne Cup, which, by itself, generates approximately 140 million Australian dollars in bets for a race that lasts seconds and creates a huge spike in online betting.[3] This spike of demand on the Melbourne Cup's website is something the site's DevOps team could not leave to the capabilities of the cloud provider; it had to come up with its own forecasting and scaling solution. Good organizations understand where they are different and define an architecture that can support them, while others just rely on the defaults provided by the cloud provider.

The second thing you need to look at is rehearsing problems. You can leverage something like Netflix's Simian Army—which consists of, among other tools, Chaos Monkey (which takes out random servers), Chaos Gorilla (which takes out entire Amazon availability zones), and Latency Monkey (which introduces artificial delays in your client server communication)—to see whether you can survive these kinds of problems.[4] Those tools can be used frequently and have increasingly become part of organizations' resilience strategies. Another strategy is to simulate a drastic catastrophe (such as an earthquake or fire—some even use alien-invasion scenarios) to stress test your resiliency and identify weakness. To be clear, these activities are not to prove that you are ready for a catastrophe but to provide opportunities to improve. The better your system gets, the more effort you put into breaking it. There is always a weakest spot, and you want to find it. Good cloud architectures are resilient to those disruptions and get better by repeatedly trying to break them. Untested resilience architectures are at the risk of failing when it matters most—during a real-life issue. In short, good cloud architecture leverages what is provided by the platform and extended by the consuming organization with additional capabilities to reflect their business and their application architecture.

First Steps for Your Organization

Review Your Cloud Applications

With the understanding of how the cloud is benefiting you most (based on the two factors—granularity of the architecture and maturity of the application in regard to DevOps practices), review your existing cloud applications (or the ones you are planning to move). To do this, first analyze the architecture to identify the components that are decoupled from each other and have the potential to be scaled independently. Also identify services that should be decoupled for later architectural refactoring. For each of the decoupled components, review their maturity of DevOps practices (SCM, build and deployment management, test automation) to identify gaps that require closing.

Next, ask yourself whether you would really benefit from the flexibility of the cloud for these applications, because you can leverage the elasticity of the architecture. Only if you have the right architecture and automation capabilities will you be able to fully benefit from the cloud. You should start building these capabilities—either before moving to the cloud or once you are in the cloud—to reduce the cost of your cloud infrastructure and the risk of business disruptions from application issues.

Based on this analysis, you will have a list of applications that are cloud ready and a backlog of work to make more and more applications cloud ready through architecture refactoring and the building of additional DevOps capabilities.

Plan a Cloud Disaster Event

Pick a scenario (e.g., your cloud provider going bust and you losing access to all the systems and data stored on the cloud) and run a full rehearsal of what it would take to come back online. This will include activities such as creating a new infrastructure with a different cloud provider, installing the applications you need to run your business, and restoring data from an external backup. There are two things that you want to do:

1. Identify your weak spots and prioritize them to improve your cloud architecture.
2. Measure the impact and duration of your rehearsal so that you can study how you become better over time.

CONCLUSION

Being a Knowledge Worker

Self-education is, I firmly believe, the only kind of education there is.
—**Isaac Asimov**, *Science Past, Science Future*

Over the course of this book, I have discussed many aspects of how organizations need to work differently to make the shift away from manufacturing thinking. This type of change is not an easy thing, and not every change I've covered is right for every organization. Furthermore, it is important that you invest the time, effort, and money necessary to do it right or you risk ending up worse off than you were before. However, the potential payoffs are enormous, and I encourage you to find ways to implement modern tech practices in your organization in any way that you can. IT work is creative work that requires knowledge workers rather than "robots" focusing on one specific task. As leaders and managers of knowledge workers, we share the mandate to stay up to date with what is happening in the industry to continue to evolve our workplace in the right direction. After all, we want to leverage all the good new technologies and practices to improve our business. We need to continuously learn.

Now that we have reached the end of the book, I want to share a bit of my personal recipes on how I deal with the requirements of continuous learning as a knowledge worker and, at the same time, share with you the resources I use to learn more. This information is for people who consider themselves knowledge workers and especially those who work with IT.

How do you manage yourself in the world of knowledge workers, where your job changes every couple of years and new tools and technologies get introduced at an ever-faster pace? Working in a modern IT organization can be scary; so many things are changing, and traditional-role definitions become less and less applicable. Agile in particular has been a real challenge for many project managers who were used to managing project plans that have been defined well in advance. All of this requires us to spend more time staying up to date than ever before. And new techniques and tools continue to appear on the collective radar faster and faster.

One thing I have learned in the last few years is that organizations can never provide all the training you need. I think Accenture's training program is one of the best in the world, with nearly all topics covered, but you want to develop broad skills and deep skills. Deep skills usually require something more than the company can provide, and completely new topics tend to take time to be adopted into your organization. So, where can you go for additional training, and what does it take?

- Conferences: Although I have learned that it is difficult to make a business case for conferences because a lot of what you learn will only play out over months, they are by far the best way to learn about new trends and get new ideas. Approaching the speaker afterward is a good way to get some of the more hard-earned lessons and hear about some of the scars that came with it. Also, be sure to make time at conferences to talk to people outside of the formal talks, to get the flip sides of the stories.
- Local meet-ups: A related activity is to attend local meet-ups. There are so many meet-ups that it can be difficult to choose which one is best. My point of view is to go to the ones that fit with your sched-

ule and mix it up. In my organization, I have appointed someone who tries to get a few people together on a regular basis, as that makes it easier for people to attend. You can combine team building and learning something new this way. And it is free. I mean, how much better can it get from a company perspective? Perhaps you should appoint a meet-up champion in your organization too.

- Massive open online courses (MOOCs) such as Coursera provide university-level courses for free. They tend to be structured around lecture videos or audio plus some activities that you should do to get the most out of the experience (including readings that can be time consuming). I have done several dozen of these, some related to work (artificial intelligence, programming, Blockchain) and others on general-interest topics, such as art and politics. It is a great way to learn something new if you can afford to spare a few hours each week.

- Open-source projects: If you have a few hours to spend but don't want to be as structured as the MOOCs are, then you can learn by contributing to an open-source project, which will allow you to learn a new technology or a new tool. I personally haven't done this in a long while; what I do instead are small home projects, where I write little programs to structure my photo collection or collect data from different sources to optimize my financial planning. I choose different technologies for these projects just to learn about these technologies. I am sure there are faster ways to achieve the outcome, but learning is, in many ways, the more important outcome than the task at hand.

- Blogs and podcasts: If you don't have that much time, then blogs and podcasts are perhaps better for you. While you can follow individual bloggers like me, a good alternative is to leverage blog aggregators such as *Dzone*, *InfoQ*, DevOps.com, or the Accenture DevOps blog, where you can read curated blog posts that cover a wider variety of topics. Podcasts are also a fantastic medium, as you can listen to those while commuting, working out, or traveling. It is a secret weapon that allows you to be somewhat productive in what is otherwise downtime. If you are like me and many others, you would probably spend that time surfing the internet or checking your email dozens of times. And you likely agree that learning something new is more useful than wasting your time with such endeavors.

- Books: Of course, there are always books to learn from. I have added a reading list to the end of this book, with my top suggestions.

Time Management

Being a new parent, writing this book (or blog posts before and after), working in consulting for a global company, and maintaining a healthy lifestyle means I am as time poor as it gets. The world of technology is moving so fast that just showing up for work means, over time, you lose contact with the latest trend. As a knowledge worker, you have to keep up to date and find the time to do that. All the things about your personal development are important; if you don't make time for them, then you will feel less and less connected with the latest trends. And as I mentioned before, I think the problem we have in the industry is partly caused by us, as leaders, not staying up to date on what has changed. We rely too much on catchy sales pitches and continuing with what we know rather than really trying to understand how all those changes play together to create a new IT and business world.

For me, every workout is an opportunity to listen to a podcast (and yes, I do not always do it; but most of the time, I resist the temptation to listen to music and choose a podcast over it); it's the same for commutes and travel. I often get a triple output by cycling to work and listening to a podcast while doing it—I get a workout, I commute to work, and I learn something new.

There are so many distractions at work, and people tend to fill your calendar with all kinds of important and not-so-important meetings. One way to avoid the day getting away from you is to schedule time for your work and your email. If you have certain activities that you need to do regularly, get them into your calendar (e.g., prepare status report, write social media post, do expense reporting). The same is true for email management; rather than doing it whenever you have time, lock in two thirty-minute slots to go through it. Lastly, put blocks of time into your calendar for your real work—time where you create that deliverable, write that code, or review someone else's work. If your highest-priority work takes time in your calendar, all the other ad hoc work can only fill the white space; and you won't find yourself doing expenses or status reports at night, because the day or week or months got away from you.

As with everything in this book, I am not trying to be prescriptive; I am under no illusion that you will follow everything I have said (as a consultant and husband, you get used to the idea that people are not following your well-meaning advice). What I hope is that with this book, you have gotten some ideas. Everything I have written comes from my experience. Like all of you, I am still learning and evolving my approach with each new project, with each new client, and with each new interaction I have with other practitioners.

There is still a lot to do to shift the IT industry into a place that is less defined by legacy thinking, as pointed out throughout this book. And new technologies and practices continue to evolve. This book will remain relevant for quite a while, I think, but we will continue to evolve; and the next generation of leaders will take a lot of today's new thinking for granted. The overall setup cost will continue to reduce (just think of Amazon Lambda functions, for example), and with that, ever-smaller batch sizes and faster speed become realistic. We will need new thinking and new management techniques to deal with the complexity that arises from so many fast-moving pieces. But let's focus on the next few steps first and evolve our solutions from there. With this book, I've given you my best guidance and access to my experience with dozens of projects and companies. I hope it will help you along your improvement journey to transform your organization. I have seen what happens when organizations improve and when people who work in IT become more engaged. It is extremely rewarding to see, and it is good for the business. You don't have to be the next Netflix or the best IT department in the country to make a real impact on your people and your business. Keep improving, and who knows? You might become a case study in your own right.

I know that you are probably very time poor, as we all are. Besides spending some money on this book, you gave me your time, which is even more valuable. Thank you! This book was a labor of love intended to make a dent in the industry we work in. I hope I will hear from you on what worked and what didn't work; it will help me continue to evolve my thinking. Feel free to reach out to me with your feedback. Perhaps we may even bump into each other at one of the conferences or a local meet-up. And if so, come say hi.

APPENDIX

A Closer Look at the Factory Analogy

Foundation Principle: Production Process in Manufacturing versus Creative Process in IT

In manufacturing, the concept is that we design a product up front, define the production process, and then produce a number of identical items. In IT, we deliver a solution that is unique to our context each time we make a change. We are never making the same product again with the same components and the same source code in the same architecture setup. Legacy manufacturing was about reducing variability. In IT, we aim to innovate by using variability to find the best solution to a problem, to the delight of our customers.

Measuring Productivity and Quality Based on Standardized Output

We have discussed that IT never delivers the same thing twice, while in manufacturing, we deliver a large number of identical items. This has significant ramifications for the measurement of productivity and quality. Let's start with the less controversial one: quality.

In manufacturing, if we are producing identical items, it is quite easy to assess quality once we have one "correct" sample or target specification. Any difference from this correct sample is a quality concern, and we can measure the number of such differences as a means to measure the quality of our production system. If there are systemic problems in the production system, fixing it once will fix the problem for all further copies of the product. Testing the manufactured product is often stochastical—we pick a number of samples from our production system to validate that the variance in production is as expected.

In IT, we don't have such "correct" samples or target specifications. We test against requirements, user stories, or design specifications, but research and experience show that these are the root causes of many defects in IT. So, our sample or target specification is often not reliable. Fixing one defect is mostly done by fixing the problem on the individual product, not by fixing the production system. As a result, the number of found defects does not necessarily say anything about the level of improvement in the production system, as we might continue to deliver the same level of "ineffective" code as before. Measuring quality in IT has to be done differently. (I talk about this in chapter 7.)

Productivity is even more difficult to measure in IT.* Truth be told, I have attended many discussions, roundtables, and talks about metrics, but so far, an appropriate measure for IT productivity has not been found by anyone I've spoken to. Many CIOs admit that they don't like whatever they are using for productivity measurement. When we put this in the context of the difference we pointed out earlier—that IT is a creative endeavor with unique outcomes in comparison to mass production in manufacturing—it becomes clear that productivity is elusive. How would you measure the pro-

---

* I elaborated in a post on my blog that productivity is very difficult to measure in IT. Instead, measure cycle time, waste, and delivered functionality.[1]

ductivity of a marketing department, an author, or a songwriter? You can measure the output (more flyers, more books, and more songs in a year), but does that make for a better marketing department, author, or songwriter?

I think you would agree that the outcome (e.g., a successful marketing campaign, bestseller, or number-one song) is, in this case, more important than the output. In the past, we have used lines of code, *function points*, and other quantifiable productivity measures, yet we all can quickly come up with reasons why those are not appropriate. With Agile, we started an obsession with story points and velocity, which are steps closer to a good answer, as they measure functionality delivered. But at its core, productivity continues to be difficult to measure. This leads to difficult discussions, especially when you are working with an IT delivery partner whom you would like to motivate to be very productive for you. (I explore some answers to this conundrum in chapter 4.)

I would love for someone to spend a bit of money to run parallel projects to see whether Agile or Waterfall, colocated or distributed, and so on can be proven to be better so that we can put that argument to rest for the holdouts that continue to argue for Waterfall delivery. In the meantime, the environment made the choice for us: the ever-faster moving market with changing requirements makes it difficult to justify doing any new work in a Waterfall manner.

Functional Specialization and Skill Set of Workers

Legacy manufacturing focused on getting the production process right by leveraging highly, narrowly specialized workers rather than focusing on the people involved in the process. IT delivery methodologies had a similar approach initially, and while a structured methodology is very beneficial. IT continues to rely on creative knowledge workers, which is different from manufacturing. The overspecialization to an assembly-like worker performing only one specific task in the IT supply chain (e.g., test or development) has proven to be suboptimal, as context is lost in highly specialized organizations. Because we are not re-creating the same solution again and again, context is extremely critical for successful delivery.

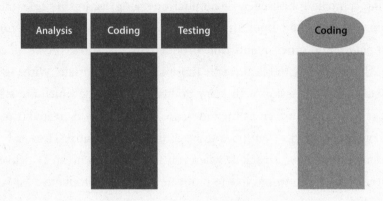

Figure A.1: T-shaped skills: T-shaped employees have broader skills than I-shaped employees

Both Agile and DevOps movements have been trying to break down the silos that exist along the SDLC to achieve a more context-aware, faster, and higher-quality organization. With this comes the transition from the ideal worker being a specialist in his field to a more broadly skilled "T-shaped" worker. T-shaped people have a working understanding of many areas and are deeply specialized in one of them, in comparison to "I-shaped" people, who know only one area.[2] The whole idea of this specialization in manufacturing was to allow less-skilled workers to perform the job of a master by relying on the production process to be prescriptive enough (designed by a skilled engineer) to make up for the difference. This, unfortunately, is not possible in IT due to the creative and complex nature of IT work.

Production Process Predictability and Governance

In manufacturing, the production process is reasonably deterministic. Once you have defined the production process and the inputs, you will get a consistent outcome. Unfortunately, this is not true in IT. Following the same methodology as another project that was successful does not guarantee you a successful outcome. There is some correlation, which is why some organizations are more successful than others, and that's the reason why certain methodologies are more widely adopted (like Scrum, SAFe, or PMBOK). But this methodology is not nearly as reliable in IT as it is in manufacturing.

This ability to predict the outcome in manufacturing means it is possible to fix a problem with a product by changing the production process. In IT, this is not the case—just changing the process does not mean it is fixed. Many change-management professionals out there will be able to testify to this.

Furthermore, the many creative inputs mean that the process itself is inherently more complex and less predictable. Governance processes that assume the same predictability as in manufacturing ultimately cause a lot of unproductive behaviors in the organization. People will "fudge" the numbers to show compliance with the predictions, but this is either done by building in enough contingency or by "massaging" the process results and leveraging the inherent ambiguities of IT. More empirical approaches like Agile allow us to show the real, less precisely predictable progress and adjust expectations accordingly. Don Reinertsen makes one of the best-articulated cases for why pretending that IT product delivery is predictable is the cause of many management problems. He explains that manufacturing is based on repetitive and predictable activities, while product delivery is inherently unique each time. Trying to use the techniques that work in a predictable delivery process in an ever-changing one will lead to failure.[3]

I discuss governance in a bit more detail in chapter 3, but let me tell you that if you see a burndown or burnup chart (Agile status reporting mechanisms) where the actuals match exactly what the original plan predicted, you've found yourself a cheater, not a predictable team.

Importance and Reliance on Upfront Planning

Due to the fact that the production process is more reliable in manufacturing than the cost of setup, it does make sense to spend more time and effort on the up-front plan. This means we can plan for a new product in manufacturing, prototype it, and then run batches and batches of the same product.

In IT, each product is different, as we identified earlier. This means we never get into the true manufacturing production process but work instead in an environment that is more comparable with the prototyping process in manufacturing. Even so, we often try to leverage the lessons learned from the production process with all its up-front planning rather than the prototyping process, which is much more incremental. As a result, we expect predictability where there is variance in outcome.

As Gary Gruver and Tommy Mouser stated in their book *Leading the Transformation: Applying Agile and DevOps Principles at Scale*, "Executives need to understand that managing software and the planning process in the same way that they manage everything else in their organization is not the most effective approach. . . . Each new software project is new and unique, so there is a higher degree of uncertainty in the planning."[4]

Governance of Delivery

Scientific management has been guiding manufacturing for a long time, and while it has been adjusted over the years, it is still the backbone of modern manufacturing. In its extreme, it means we are happy to govern delivery of components at the end of the process; for example, we are happy for the actual delivery to be a black box as long as the end product is exactly the product we specified. Because the specification is a lot more objective too, we can rely on this process.

NOT LIKE THIS

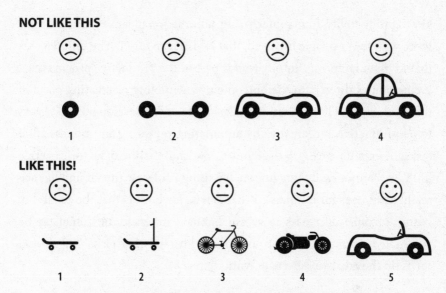

LIKE THIS!

Figure A.2: Iterative versus incremental delivery: Iterative delivery slowly increases the benefits of the product, while incremental requires the full product before it is useful

(Recreated based on image by Henrik Kniberg, "Making Sense of MVP (Minimum Viable Product)—and why I prefer Earliest Testable/Usuable/Lovable," *Crisp's* Blog, January 25, 2016, http://blog.crisp.se/2016/01/25/henrik kniberg/making-sense-of-MVP.)

In IT, the specification is less clear; it's the governance that needs to be a lot more transparent. Over the years, Agile has shown that the cone of uncertainty can be significantly reduced by building small increments of working software that can be evaluated at each iteration. This is not really possible in manufacturing, as building multiple iterations of a car is much harder than building multiple iterations of a website. So, in manufacturing, we will continue to rely on incremental build-and-progress reporting, while IT takes a more iterative build-and-progress approach. Figure A.2 nicely shows the difference between incremental and iterative delivery, using the example of building a vehicle.

Automation Is Productivity

Automation is one aspect where both manufacturing and IT delivery have a common goal: automate as much as possible. Automation is really the key to productivity. In manufacturing, automation means we can produce more with fewer people involved; that is also true for IT. The difference is that in manufacturing, automation is part of the productive process (e.g., it contributes directly to the outcome by assembling or creating parts of the product). In IT, automation makes it easier for developers and testers to be productive and creative by automating repeating and nonessential tasks. In manufacturing, we see end-to-end automation of factories, while in IT, we cannot easily imagine such a thing (unless artificial intelligence really takes over for humans). What is true for both is that the reliability of the outcomes decreases as we use manual workers for tasks that can be automated. Humans are just not good with repeating tasks and should focus on the creative aspects of work.

Scaling Efforts to Deliver More

Everything we have said so far—a more deterministic production process, less reliability on skilled workers, and differences in the predictability of outcome—means that scaling up manufacturing is something we have mastered over the years. You build another factory and hire workers, and you have a good chance of producing a similar product—even with all the possible cultural or logistical challenges.

In IT, scaling increases the complexity of the production process significantly more than it increases in manufacturing. There are more parties that need to communicate, information needs to be disseminated more widely, and common context needs to be created across more communication boundaries. The cost of this additional scale is quite significant in IT. Yet IT systems continue to grow, and we have to find ways to deal with this apart from adding more people. We want IT systems to solve big problems, so we need better scaling approaches. Great work has been done to show that adding people to a project in trouble does not improve the outcome but makes it worse. Frederick Brooks describes how, in IBM, adding more programmers to a project did not make it faster but delayed it further.[5] Or as he so poignantly summarizes it, "The bearing of a child takes nine months, no matter how many women are assigned."[6] Being able to do more with the same amount of people while still making systems easier to maintain are the answers that Agile and DevOps practitioners prefer over just adding more people.

Centralization of Resources

Factories were a mechanism to provide economies of scale. Central production resources like the manufacturing machines and the input material were stored in central places so that the workforce could have easy access to them and produce in the most efficient way. In IT, this was initially true too. You had to have access to powerful computing resources, and later, good internet connections. Today, this is all available to you from pretty much anywhere thanks to broadband and the cloud. This means location should not be driven by resources but by the need for communication and skill-set available. How do you bring the right team together to deliver the outcome you are trying to achieve? There is some centralization of resources that still makes sense (e.g., providing easy-to-use developer tools and standardized environments), but it has become a lot less necessary over time and, certainly, less location specific.

Offshoring

Offshoring in manufacturing was an appropriate way of reducing the economic footprint. The production process could be replicated offshore, and the variation in outcome was somewhat controllable. In IT, too often, the same principle was applied without consciously recognizing that context is extremely important for IT delivery to be successful; and accordingly, the communication channels need to be excellent to achieve the same outcome. Offshoring is still an appropriate way to extend your IT capabilities, especially when scale is required. To leverage wage arbitrage, delivering the same project with a colocated team onshore or with distributed teams across the world is probably going to cost you roughly the same. Distribution tends to slow things down due to the communication lag; hence, distributed projects tend to take longer. In many cases, onshore colocated teams are not an option, though, as the required skills or amount of engineers are not available. Then, offshore capabilities are required to deliver complex projects. Unfortunately, many IT executives still see offshoring as a cost-reduction exercise rather than a capability extension, which causes a lot of the problems that created offshore delivery's somewhat mixed reputation.

Outsourcing

Outsourcing IT is a lot more difficult than outsourcing manufacturing. In manufacturing, you outsource the production of specific components, and as long as the specifications are adhered to, you are happy. You can control the output pretty well too, as there is a concrete item being produced.

Outsourcing IT is a lot harder. The specifications in IT are much more complex and less set in stone. We know that many quality problems come from bad requirements, and no project gets completed without stakeholders changing their mind on something. Given that we cannot easily determine the product of the relationship and evaluate the outcome, we need to care about the process. An outsourcing partner in IT should provide you with capability you don't have in-house, either in skills or experience, and they should be transparent and collaborative in their approach, as you will have to work through the complex project delivery together. Only when both sides win can the project be successful. Think about what that means in regard to the commercial construct and the people strategy for both sides. Too many IT outsourcing arrangements are adversarial in their setup and either deteriorate quickly or cause everyone to walk a fine line. I have been lucky that I have been working with some great organizations who collaborated with me to identify a mutually beneficial structure to deliver projects.

What I hope is clear is that the ideas that got us here and made us successful in the past require some rethinking and adjustment to continue to work for us. Rather than thinking of labor-intensive legacy manufacturing factories, we need to operate more like highly automated factories. And I think the DevOps movement is a great catalyst for this required change in thinking.

Resources

Books

Continuous Delivery: Reliable Software Releases through Build, Test, and Deployment Automation by Jez Humble and David Farley: a very technical reference book on how to implement continuous delivery

Leading the Transformation: Applying Agile and DevOps Principles at Scale by Gary Gruver and Tommy Mouser: a great book with very pragmatic advice on how to start the transformation for IT.

The DevOps Handbook: How to Create World-Class Agility, Reliability, and Security in Technology Organizations by Gene Kim, Jez Humble, Patrick Debois, and John Willis: this book provides a lot of useful guidance on implementing DevOps practices.

The Effective Manager by Mark Horstman: this is a great book on good management that focuses on the people who work for you.

The Goal: A Process of Ongoing Improvement by Eliyahu M. Goldratt and Jeff Cox: an easy-to-read business novel introducing you to systems thinking

The Lean Startup: How Today's Entrepreneurs Use Continuous Innovation to Create Radically Successful Businesses by Eric Ries: Eric describes how structured experimentation allows you to better solve business problems.

The Phoenix Project: A Novel About IT, DevOps, and Helping Your Business Win by Gene Kim, Kevin Behr, and George Spafford: this one is an easy-to-read novel introducing you to DevOps concepts and culture.

The Principles of Product Development Flow: Second Generation Lean Product Development by Donald G. Reinertsen: a great book including some of the best discussion of batch size

Site Reliability Engineering: How Google Runs Production Systems by Betsy Beyer, Chris Jones, Jennifer Petoff and Niall Richard Murphy: learn about modern operations for applications inspired by Google.

Podcasts and Online Resources

The Agile Revolution: an Australia-based Agile podcast (TheAgileRevolution.com)

Arrested DevOps: a podcast that provides information on upcoming conferences as well as discussion on DevOps topics (ArrestedDevOps.com)

Career Tools: a helpful podcast from Manager Tools designed to offer advice to anyone at any point on their career path (https://www.manager-tools.com/all-podcasts?field_content_domain_tid=5)

DevOps Café: a conversational-style podcast about all things DevOps (DevOpsCafe.org)

The Economist Radio: a daily podcast for staying up to date with science and politics (https://radio.economist.com/)

Freakonomics Radio: a podcast of surprising insights from science into the world around us (http://freakonomics.com/archive/)

HBR IdeaCast: a business-focused podcast from *Harvard Business Review* that dives deep into one specific area per episode (http://feeds.har vardbusiness.org/harvardbusiness/ideacast)

Manager Tools: great guidance for managers and directors (https://www .manager-tools.com/all-podcasts?field_content_domain_tid=4)

The Ship Show (now defunct, but episodes are still out there): one of the earlier DevOps podcasts (TheShipShow.com)

Software Engineering Radio: an in-depth podcast on technical topics (http://www.se-radio.net/)

TED Talks: inspirational talks that often cover science and technology (https://www.ted.com/talks)

Glossary

abstract environment configuration: variables like IP addresses and server names need to be abstracted so that configuration files only contain placeholders and not the actual values.

abstraction layer: an abstraction layer decouples two layers of architecture so that they can evolve independently from each other without being tightly coupled and causing dependencies.

access layer: usually a user interface that makes accessing information in the underlying systems easier and more user friendly than direct-access systems.

application programming interface (API): is a set of clearly defined methods of communication between various software components that allows access to functionality from external systems.

average daily rate (ADR): the average cost for a day of work across a team of resources with several daily cost rates per person.

bimodal IT: a concept introduced to demonstrate that newer, more modern IT systems are being developed differently from older systems.

black box mode: a type of IT delivery for which the customer does not care about the means of delivery and is only interested in the outcome.

blameless postmortem: a review technique that focuses on systematic problems and is purposefully not looking to attach blame to an individual.

build artifacts: the result of the build process, often as a binary that can then be used to deploy an application.

business IT isomorphism: the organizational approach to align IT functions with business functions to simplify the engagement model between business and IT.

canary testing: inspired by the canary in the coal mine, this approach deploys into a subset of production to validate the application before rolling it out more widely.

cloud: the practice of using a network of remote servers hosted on the internet to store, manage, and process data rather than using a local server.

cloud native application: an application built specifically to leverage the abilities of cloud computing and hence be more resilient and efficient.

compilers: utilities that "translate" programming code into executable programs.

compute environments: application environments that allow you to execute programs.

concept of error budgets: budgets that, instead of the more traditional costs, allocate a level of errors or outages to teams that they have to manage in order to be seen as successful.

configuration drift: when a server configuration starts to drift away from its intended configuration by either human or system intervention.

consumable services: IT services that can be called upon by other programs and that provide easy-to-consume interfaces as a contract of engagement.

container images: representations of an application in a container that can be deployed into a container engine for fast creation of the application.

continuous delivery: an IT practice made popular by a book of the same name in which software is automatically evaluated for quality and deployed into environments all the way up to production.

continuous integration: is a development practice that requires developers to integrate code into a shared repository several times a day. Each check-in is then verified by an automated build, allowing teams to detect problems early.

cost performance indicator (CPI): a metric that allows you to measure how much work has been performed for a certain amount of cost.

COTS product: commercial-off-the-shelf products are preconfigured IT applications that support certain business processes without much configuration or programming required.

CRM system: a customer relationship management system allows a company to engage with its customers in a consistent way and leverage the relationships for further business cutover.

cycle time: the total time from the beginning to the end of your process, as defined by you and your customer.

dashboard: a visualization of several data points or reports aggregated across several data sources so that the information is easily available.

decoupling of systems: a technique that enables systems to be changed independently from each other by introducing interfaces that remain stable when each of the systems changes.

defect density: a metric that measures how many defects per day of programming or line of code are introduced.

definition of done: an Agile practice that defines the exit criteria under which user stories are considered to be done. (See also *definition of ready*.)

definition of ready: an Agile practice that defines the entry criteria for user stories to be considered for the next sprint. (See also *definition of done*.)

develop-operate-transition (DOT) contracts: a popular contract structure that differentiates between vendors who deliver a solution, vendors who operate the solution, and the state in which the organization transitions the solution back in-house.

DevOps tool chains: the set of tools that supports DevOps practices like configuration management, deployment automation, and test automation, among others.

discovery: a phase in the beginning of an Agile project used to align all stakeholders on the intended outcome of the project and the way the team will achieve this.

discovery showcase: a meeting at the end of discovery in which the results of the phase are shared with a broader set of stakeholders.

end-state architecture: the envisioned end state of the application architecture that will fully support the business of an organization.

ERP system: an enterprise resource planning system is the practice of managing all the resources for the production and fulfillment process of an organization.

front-end team: the team that delivers the front-end experience with which the end customers interact.

function call: the programming technique that allows the usage of functions provided by other applications or parts of the same application.

function points: an estimation technique that aims to provide an objective way to measure work in IT projects.

go-live: the release of new functionality or a new program when it is ready for customer use.

graceful degradation: a practice that allows systems to provide basic functionality even when core processes are not available; this is in contrast to being completely unavailable when one function fails.

green field setting: a project setting in which the team can start from scratch instead of having to consider existing applications.

hardening: an Agile project phase right before production deployment in which additional testing (such as performance and security testing) takes place that was not able to be accommodated in the Agile sprints.

horizontal scaling: a scaling technique in which additional workflows are distributed to more systems of the same size and shape instead of providing more resources to the same systems.

IDE extensions: extensions that are provided for developers in their integrated development environment to support specific programming languages with helpful utilities.

internet natives: companies that were built around solutions that leverage the internet and hence considered internet capabilities in the application architecture from the inception of the service.

iterative character: something that evolves over several iterations, with each iteration bringing it closer to the real answer.

Jenkins: a continuous-integration tool.

lead time: the time between the initiation and the completion of a production process.

legacy: in the context of IT, this describes applications that were built in the past and need to be maintained.n (See also *true legacy*.)

LeSS: Large-Scale Scrum, a scaling method for Agile.

mean time to discovery (MTTD): the mean time it takes to identify that a problem exists. (See also *mean time to recovery*.)

mean time to recovery (MTTR): the mean time it takes to rectify a problem. (See also *mean time to discovery*.)

mental models: the models that humans use to understand the world and make decisions, often leveraging heuristics, as too much information is available for full evaluation.

microservices: an architecture paradigm that tries to identify the smallest possible independent component that can run as a service.

middleware: software that runs in between the operating system and applications (i.e., integration services and data access layers).

minimum viable cluster: the minimum set of applications that can be changed so that a real positive impact can be made by uplifting the DevOps capabilities.

minimum viable product (MVP): a product that has only the absolute necessary features to validate its viability with customers. Additional scope is then built out over time.

monolithic applications: applications that provide many different services that can only be deployed together.

multimodal IT: an IT environment that leverages several modes of delivery across the Agile and Waterfall spectrum.

NPS: the net promoter score is a metric that measures the satisfaction of a constituency with a service provider or organization.

open source: a software distribution model that does not require payment for usage and is based largely on voluntary contribution to the source code.

Perl: a scripting language often used for automating tasks.

PI planning: program increment planning is an implementation of large-room planning in the Scaled Agile framework, which brings all stake-holders together for a combined planning event of the next planning cycle.

PMI: Project Management Institute runs a training and certification program for project managers.

program increment: a planning duration that consists of several sprints/iterations. Usually consists of around five sprints and is around three months long.

pulling model: an interaction model between services in which the consuming service pulls information rather than providing a queue in which the production service pushes information.

queuing theory: a scientific approach to understanding how queues behave.

refactoring: a programming practice that allows programmers to improve the structure of a program without making functional changes.

regression suite: a set of tests that ensure that previously implemented functionality continues to work.

release train: a superstructure (team of teams) that delivers to a common outcome, usually a team of 3–12 Agile teams.

robotic process automation (RPA): a tooling technique that provides utilities to automate tasks in applications that would otherwise have to be performed manually by human beings.

scale up/vertical: scaling techniques that add additional compute or other services to the same instance instead of distributing workflows to additional instances.

Scaled Agile Framework (SAFe): a popular scaling framework for Agile delivery.

schedule performance indicator (SPI): a metric measuring whether or not a project is on schedule according to a predefined plan.

shell scripts: a popular automation technique based on the UNIX shell.

site reliability engineering: a modern operations approach made popular by Google.

software as a service (SaaS): software that is provided as a service from the cloud and in a per-consumption model.

software configuration management: is the practice of tracking and controlling changes in software that includes version control, branching of parallel development, and maintaining a view of what versions of code are included in a software package.

software delivery life cycle (SDLC): this cycle describes all activities required to implement requirements from idea to production go-live.

stateful calls: a programming technique that requires a service to remember the state of the transaction to successfully complete it over several transactions.

stateless calls: a programming technique that does not require a service to know the current state of the transaction.

story points: a sizing approach in Agile methods that is based on relative sizing instead of absolute sizes, such as days or hours.

strangler pattern: a programming technique that builds new functionality and diverts workflows to the new functionality incrementally until the old program can be turned off.

systems integrator (SI): a company that helps organizations to bring the different components of a system together through implementing, planning, coordinating, scheduling, testing, improving, and sometimes maintaining the system for the organization.

systems of engagement: systems that users directly engage with and that evolve quickly. (See also *systems of record*.)

systems of record: systems that hold core data and do not need to evolve quickly. (See also *systems of engagement*.)

systems thinking: an approach to analyzing systems as a whole instead of as a sum of their parts.

technical debt: known or unknown parts of programs that are currently suboptimal and should be refactored.

technology stack: all the technologies that are required to support business functions from the operating system up to the actual applications.

telematics: a systematic approach to gathering and using information that is generated during the use of a system.

theory of constraints: a scientific approach to analyzing systems based on the constraints that exist in the system.

to-be process design: the planned state of a process to be implemented that improves on the current condition.

true legacy: systems that are not being updated anymore and are only kept running to support business functions. (See also *legacy*.)

twelve-factor application: an architecture concept that provides twelve criteria for modern applications.

two-speed delivery model: a model that supports two different speeds of delivery to differentiate between fast-changing and slow-changing systems.

upskilling time: the time required for new people to become effective when joining a new team or learning a new skill.

user stories: used in Agile methods to describe the functionality of the system, often in the format of "As a <role>, I want to <functionality> so that <outcome>."

value stream mapping: an activity that maps out the whole legacy tranformation to support a process including contextual information such as timings, tooling, and other actors.

versioning: the practice of storing multiple versions of a program or other artifact so that it is possible to move between known states of configuration.

walled-garden test automation tools: test automation tools that are not enabled through application programming interfaces and that are only possible to be used within a specific technology or vendor context.

Waterfall: an exaggerated delivery approach based on stage containment between requirement, design, development, and test.

weighted shortest job first: is a way to determine the sequence of work by dividing the value one derives from the work by the cost of the work. An example formula for this is based on SAFe: cost of delay/duration.

XaaS: anything as a service.

Index

Note: In this index, *f* stands for figure, *n* stands for note, and *t* stands for table.

IT delivery, (*continued*)
approvals and reviews, 21–22
dashboards, 15
deployment approval processes, 20–21
deployment lead time, 21–22
deployment pipeline, 15, 16–17*f*
governance cost, 22
governance process step examination, 21–22
and manufacturing principles, xxvi–xxix
process diagrams, 4
IT delivery process diagrams, 4
IT governance, 17–20, 25–26
analytics solutions, 19
annotated snapshots, 19*f*
bottlenecks, 20
dashboards, 20
objective measures, 18
project managers, 18
status reports, 18
iterative character, 86
iterative *vs.* incremental delivery, 215*f*

J
Jenkins, 12, 91

K
KISS, 167
knowledge workers, 203–208
blogs and podcasts, 205–206
books, 206
conferences, 204
local meet-ups, 204–205
massive open online courses, 205
open-source projects, 205
time management, 206–208
training, 203–205
Koçulu, Azer, 194
KPIs, 138, 139

L
large business cases *vs.* smaller initial steps, 14
Large-Scale Scrum (LeSS), 62
latency, 169
Latency Monkey, 200
layers, 167, 169, 170
lead time, 21, 162
*Leading the Transformation: Applying Agile and
    DevOps Principles at Scale* (Gruver and Mouser),
    214
Lean treatment and IT, 20–26
approvals and reviews, 21–22
deployment lead time, 21–22
governance cost, 22
governance process step examination, 21–22
legacy applications, 27–43, 52–56
application portfolio analysis, 27, 29–31, 40–42, 42*t*

application radar, 31*f*
big bang transformations, 28
bimodal IT, 28
business support applications, 30
checkpoint 1, 36–37
checkpoint 2, 37–38
checkpoint 3, 38–39
checkpoint 4, 39
commercial-off-the-shelf products, 30
creative techniques to manage, 56
customer-facing applications, 30
end-state architecture, 35
fast digital *vs.* slow enterprise applications, 28
governance checkpoints, 35–39, 36*f*
innovation engine applications, 30
minimum viable cluster, 31–33, 33*f*, 42–43
multimodal IT, 28–29
prioritization of applications, 31–33
reducing investment in application, 54–55
strangler pattern, 34, 54–55
surfacing the real cost of, 34–35
system integrators, 53
technical debt, 28
true legacy applications, 29–30, 31*f*, 34–35, 74
user groups, 53–54
vendor incentivization, 55
legacy architecture, xxiv
LeSS, 62
Lewis, James, 173
limited resource consumption, 168
local meet-ups, 204–205
logical environment management, 196
logs, 198

M
management and measurements, 127–128
Manager Tools (podcast), 135
managers, 131–140
blameless culture, 136–137
culture KPIs, 139
delegation, 135–136
feedback, 134–135
measuring organization culture, 137–138
one-on-ones, 133–134, 138–139
people as resources, 131–132
managing dependencies, 194
managing evolving tool sets, 185–186
manual peer reviews, 122
manufacturing approach to delivery, 82
mapping, 163
massive open online courses, 205
mastery, 91
mean time to discovery (MTTD), 198
mean time to recovery (MTTR), 198
*Measure Efficiency, Effectiveness, and Culture to
    Optimize DevOps Transformation*, 137

Notes

Preface

1. Mirco Hering, "Agile Reporting at the Enterprise Level (Part 2)—Measuring Productivity," *Not a Factory Anymore* (blog), February 26, 2015, https://notafactoryanymore.com/2015/02/26/agile-reporting-at-the-enterprise-level-part-2-measuring-productivity.

Introduction

1. Stefan Thomke and Donald Reinertsen, "Six Myths of Product Development," *Harvard Business Review*, May 2012, https://hbr.org/2012/05/six-myths-of-product-development.
2. Don Reinertsen, "Thriving in a Stochastic World," speech, YOW! conference, December 7, 2015, Brisbane, Australia, YouTube video, 56:49, posted by "YOW! Conferences," December 25, 2015, https://www.youtube.com/watch?v=wyZNxB172VI.
3. "The Lean Startup Methodology," The Lean Startup (website), accessed November 10, 2017, http://theleanstartup.com/principles.
4. Brad Power, "How GE Applies Lean Startup Practices," *Harvard Business Review*, April 23, 2014, https://hbr.org/2014/04/how-ge-applies-lean-startup-practices.
5. Mirco Hering, "Let's Burn the Software Factory to the Ground—and from Their Ashes Software Studios Shall Rise," *Not a Factory Anymore* (blog), November 9, 2015,

https://notafactoryanymore.com/2015/11/09/lets-burn-the-software-factory-to-the
-ground-and-from-their-ashes-software-studios-shall-rise.

6. Mark Rendell, "Breaking the 2 Pizza Paradox with Platform Applications," speech, DevOps Enterprise Summit 2015, San Francisco, CA, YouTube video, 25:26, posted by "DevOps Enterprise Summit," November 10, 2015, https://www.youtube.com /watch?v=8WRRi6oui34.

Chapter 1

1. "The DevOps Platform: Overview," ADOP (Accenture DevOps Platform on GitHub), Accenture, accessed May 2, 2017, http://accenture.github.io/adop-docker-compose.

2. Carreth Read, *Logic: Deductive and Inductive* (London: DeLaMare Press, 1909), 320.

Chapter 2

1. "Gartner IT Glossary: Bimodal," Gartner, Inc., accessed May 2, 2017, http://www.gart-ner.com/it-glossary/bimodal.

2. Ted Schadler, "A Billion Smartphones Require New Systems of Engagement," Forrester Research, Inc. blogs, February 14, 2012, http://blogs.forrester.com/ted_schadler/12 -02-14-a_billion_smartphones_require_new_systems_of_engagement.

3. Martin Fowler, "Strangler Application," *MartinFowler.com* (blog), June 29, 2004, http:// www.martinfowler.com/bliki/StranglerApplication.html.

Chapter 3

1. Mirco Hering, "How to Deal with COTS Products in a DevOps World," *InfoQ* (blog), July 24, 2016, https://www.infoq.com/articles/cots-in-devops-world.

Chapter 4

1. Francis Keany, "Census Outage Could Have Been Prevented by Turning Router On and Off Again: IBM," ABC News, October 25, 2016, http://www.abc.net.au/news/2016-10-25 /turning-router-off-and-on-could-have-prevented-census-outage/7963916.

2. Mike Masnick, "Contractors Who Built Healthcare.gov Website Blame Each Other for All the Problems," *Techdirt* (blog), October 24, 2013, https://www.techdirt.com /articles/20131023/18053424992/contractors-who-built-healthcaregov-website -blame-each-other-all-problems.shtml.

Part B Introduction

1. Barry Schwartz, "The Way We Think about Work Is Broken," filmed March 2014 in Vancouver, BC, TED video, 7:42, https://www.ted.com/talks/barry_schwartz _the_way_we_think_about_work_is_broken.
2. Dan Pink, "The Puzzle of Motivation," filmed July 2009 in Oxford, England, TED video, 18:36, https://www.ted.com/talks/dan_pink_on_motivation.

Chapter 5

1. "PI Planning," SAFe (Scaled Agile Framework), Scaled Agile, Inc., updated November 11, 2017, http://www.scaledagileframework.com/pi-planning.
2. Paul Ellarby, "Using Big Room Planning to Help Plan a Project with Many Teams," *TechWell Insights* (blog), November 26, 2014, https://www.techwell.com/techwell -insights /2014/11/using-big-room-planning-help-plan-project-many-teams.
3. Wikipedia, s.v. "Dunning–Kruger effect," last modified November 11, 2017, 19:01, https://en.wikipedia.org/wiki/Dunning%E2%80%93Kruger_effect.
4. Wikipedia, s.v. "Technology tree," last modified November 13, 2017, 21:45, https:// en.wikipedia.org/wiki/Technology_tree.

Chapter 6

1. Jargon File (version 4.4.7), s.v. "Conway's Law," accessed November 14, 2017, http:// catb.org/~esr/jargon/html/C/Conways-Law.html.
2. *2016 State of DevOps Report* (Portland, OR: Puppet Labs, 2016), p. 9, https://puppet .com/resources/white-paper/2016-state-of-devops-report.
3. Rouan Wilsenach, "DevOpsCulture," *MartinFowler.com* (blog), July 9, 2015, https:// martinfowler.com/bliki/DevOpsCulture.html.
4. Matthew Skelton, "What Team Structure Is Right for DevOps to Flourish?" ed. Manuel Pais, *DevOps Topologies* (blog), accessed May 2, 2017, http://web.devopstopologies .com.
5. "WSJF—Weighted Shortest Job First," Black Swan Farming, accessed May 2, 2017, http://blackswanfarming.com/wsjf-weighted-shortest-job-first.

Chapter 7

1. W. Edwards Deming, *Out of the Crisis* (Cambridge, MA: MIT Press, 1982), 29.

2. Kin Lane, "The Secret to Amazon's Success Internal APIs," API Evangelist blog, January 12, 2012, http://apievangelist.com/2012/01/12/the-secret-to-amazons -success -internal-apis.

3. Jeff Galimore et al., *Tactics for Implementing Test Automation for Legacy Code* (Portland, OR: IT Revolution, 2015).

Chapter 8

1. Anonymous, private conversation with author, 2004.

2. Dan Pink, "The Puzzle of Motivation," filmed July 2009 in Oxford, England, TED video, 18:36, https://www.ted.com/talks/dan_pink_on_motivation.

3. Mark Horstman, "Managerial Economics 101," YouTube video, 4:33, posted by "Manager Tools," May 3, 2009, https://www.youtube.com/watch?v=gP-RC5ZqiBg.

4. John Goulah, "Making It Virtually Easy to Deploy on Day One," *Code as Craft* (blog), March 13, 2012, https://codeascraft.com/2012/03/13/making-it-virtually-easy-to -deploy-on-day-one.

5. Mirco Hering, Dominica DeGrandis, and Nicole Forsgren, *Measure Efficiency, Effectiveness, and Culture to Optimize DevOps Transformation* (Portland, OR: IT Revolution, 2015), 14, https://itrevolution.com/book/measure-efficiency-effectiveness -culture-optimize-devops-transformations.

Chapter 9

1. Jez Humble and David Farley, *Continuous Delivery: Reliable Software Releases through Build, Test, and Deployment Automation* (Crawfordsville, IN: Pearson Education, Inc., 2011).

2. *The Netflix Tech Blog*, assessed November 16, 2017, http://techblog.netflix.com.

3. "Hygieia: An OSS Project Sponsored by Capital One," Capital One DevExchange, assessed November 16, 2017, https://developer.capitalone.com/opensource-projects /hygieia.

Chapter 10

1. Jez Humble, "Architecting for Continuous Delivery," speech, DevOps Enterprise Summit 2015, San Francisco, CA, YouTube video, 34:17, posted by "DevOps Enterprise Summit," November 17, 2015, https://www.youtube.com/watch?v=_wnd-eyPoMo.

2. Randy Shoup, "Pragmatic Microservices: Whether, When, and How to Migrate," speech, YOW! conference, December 2015, Brisbane, Australia, YouTube video,

49:00, posted by "YOW! Conferences," December 30, 2015, https://www.youtube.com/watch?v=hAwpVXiLH9M.

3. James Lewis, "Microservices—Building Software That Is #Neverdone," speech, YOW! conference, December 2015, Brisbane, Australia, YouTube video, 45:55, posted by "YOW! Conferences," December 29, 2015, https://www.youtube.com/watch?v=JEtxmsJzrnw.

4. Wikipedia, c.v. "Conway's law," last modified November 3, 2017, 09:02, https://en.wikipedia.org/wiki/Conway%27s_law.

Chapter 11

1. "About IT4IT," The Open Group, accessed August 4, 2017, http://www.opengroup.org/IT4IT/overview.

Chapter 12

1. Keith Collins, "How One Programmer Broke the Internet by Deleting a Tiny Piece of Code," Quartz Media, March 27, 2016, https://qz.com/646467/how-one-programmer-broke-the-internet-by-deleting-a-tiny-piece-of-code.

2. Josh Corman and John Willis, "Immutable Awesomeness," speech, DevOps Enterprise Summit 2015, San Francisco, CA, YouTube video, 34:25, posted by "Sonatype," October 21, 2015, https://www.youtube.com/watch?v=-S8-lrm3iV4.

3. Debbi Schipp, "Bonus Bet Offers Peak as Online Agencies Chase Cup Day Dollars," News.com.au, November 1, 2016, http://www.news.com.au/sport/superracing/melbourne-cup/bonus-bet-offers-peak-as-online-agencies-chase-cup-day-dollars/news-story/8e09a39396fb5485cf1f24cbea228ff9.

4. Yury Izrailevsky and Ariel Tseitlin, "The Netflix Simian Army," *The Netflix Tech Blog*, July 18, 2011, http://techblog.netflix.com/2011/07/netflix-simian-army.html.

Appendix

1. Mirco Hering, "Agile Reporting at the Enterprise Level (Part 2)—Measuring Productivity," *Not a Factory Anymore* (blog), February 26, 2015, https://notafactoryanymore.com/2015/02/26/agile-reporting-at-the-enterprise-level-part-2-measuring-productivity.

2. Andy Boynton and William Bole, "Are You an 'I' or a 'T'?" *Forbes Leadership* (blog), October 18, 2011http://www.forbes.com/sites/andyboynton/2011/10/18/are-you-an-i-or-a-t/#2517d 45b351b.

3. Don Reinertsen, "Thriving in a Stochastic World," speech, YOW! conference, December 7, 2015, Brisbane, Australia, YouTube video, 56:50 posted by "YOW! Conferences," December 25, 2015, https://www.youtube.com/watch?v=wyZNxB172VI.

4. Gary Gruver and Tommy Mouser, *Leading the Transformation: Applying Agile and DevOps Principles at Scale* (Portland, OR: IT Revolution, 2015), 17.

5. Frederick P. Brooks, Jr., *The Mythical Man-Month: Essays on Software Engineering*, anniversary ed., 2nd ed., (Crawfordsville, IN: Addison-Wesley Longman, Inc., 2010), 25.

6. Brooks, *The Mythical Man-Month*, 17.

Acknowledgments

Like they say about raising children, the same is true for writing a book—it takes a village to do so. And I am sure I will miss people who should really be on these pages. Apologies for that. Grab me at the next conference, and I will buy you a drink instead.

First of all, I have to thank the fantastic team that supported me through the editing process: Todd, Gene, Anna, Leah, and Karen—without you, my thoughts would have never found a presentable and readable form. It was hard work but also a lot of fun working with you.

Then there are the peer reviewers who offered up some of their valuable time to provide feedback: Eric, Yong, Ajay, and Emily—you helped to bring the book into final shape and kept me honest.

I have some special thanks to give to three people without whom this book would have never happened: Eric, Todd, and Gene—you helped me move from "I can never write a meaningful book" to "Hey, I might have something to say that can help people." Your early support kicked off all of this.

I want to thank Accenture leadership—Bhaskar Ghosh, Adam Burden, and Peter Vakkas—for their support of this project and for providing me the flexibility at work to get this "labor of love" done.

And then there is Gary Gruver, who shared many pieces of advice from his book-writing experience and helped me come up with my own writing strategy.

I would also like to thank all the people in the Accenture DevOps practice and other parts of the company who helped shape my approach to enterprise transformations. I want to thank the clients that I have been working with and from whom I always learn something new during the engagements. You might find some of your thinking reflected in this book.

Last but not least, I need to say a huge thank you to my wife, Anjali, who has been a fantastic support as I have been writing this book—and at a time in our life that already has a full schedule thanks to a beautiful little boy, who was born while this book was in progress. Anjali, you are an absolute star!

About the Author

For over a dozen years, Mirco Hering has worked on accelerating software delivery through innovative approaches (what is now called DevOps), and ten years ago, started experimenting with Agile methods. As the Asia Pacific lead for DevOps and Agile at Accenture, he supports major public- and private-sector companies around the world in their search for efficient IT delivery. Mirco blogs about his experiences at NotAFactoryAnymore.com and speaks at global conferences to share what he has learned. You can also follow Mirco on Twitter: @MircoHering.